Also by asha bandele

Fiction and Poetry

Daughter
The Subtle Art of Breathing
Absence in the Palms of My Hand

Nonfiction

The Prisoner's Wife

something

something like beautiful

One Single Mother's Story

asha bandele

COLLINS

An Imprint of HarperCollins Publishers

For Nisa, daughter and inspiration

AND

For Victoria, agent and midwife

HarperCollins books may be purchased for educational, business, or sales promotional use. For information, please write: Special Markets Department, HarperCollins Publishers, 10 East 53rd Street, New York, NY 10022.

FIRST EDITION

Designed by Renato Stanisic

Library of Congress Cataloging-in-Publication Data

Bandele, Asha.
   Something like beautiful: one single mother's story/Asha Bandele.—1st ed.
p. cm.
ISBN 978-0-06-171037-7
   1. Bandele, Asha. 2. African American single mothers—Biography. 3. African American single mothers—Social conditions. 4. Single mothers—United States—Biography. 5. Single mothers—Social conditions. 6. Motherhood—United States—Case studies. I. Title.

HQ759.915.B36 2008
306.874'32092—dc22

                                                                2008022024

09 10 11 12 13   OV/RRD   10 9 8 7 6 5 4 3 2 1

If you want to understand any woman you must first ask about her mother and then listen carefully . . . Wistful silences demonstrate unfinished business. The more a daughter knows the details of her mother's life—without flinching or whining—the stronger the daughter.

ANITA DIAMANT, *The Red Tent*

love in a time of confinement

This is a book about love and this is a book about rage. This is a book about those opposing emotions and what happens to a woman, a mother, when, with equal weight, they occupy the seat of your heart. This is a book about what happened when they occupied the seat of mine at the very time when all I should have known, all I was told I should have known, was joy. Because what else is there but joy when a mother is staring into the brilliant eyes of the daughter she dreamed of, prayed for, and finally, finally made manifest? My laughter in those hours, days, weeks, and early months when Nisa was new and in my arms, on my breast, then, my laughter was loud, raucous even. It was regular and it was unbidden.

And then everything changed, dipped down so very, very low, but this is not a story about postpartum depression. It's an everyday life story of an everyday mother.

It's a story about the orbit of sadness that begins spinning in you and around you when you discover that the great life and love you had put together, the emotional balance and financial wherewithal, nearly everything you had counted on— everything I had counted on—disappeared, or, perhaps more accurately, shifted just out of focus. You can still make it out, sort of, what the picture was, but you have to squint. And even then, blurs.

The particulars of my own life involve prisons and no parole, single parenting, and shaky finances. But in a sense, they don't matter, my particulars. What I know now, after all these years trying to climb out of a hole, is that I am part of a long line of women, Black women especially, who believe we have no right to pain, rage, sadness, that to acknowledge them, let alone walk all the way into them, walk all the way into the feelings so we can at last deconstruct them, is weak, weird, wrong, just plain wrong. But when we banish them, send them out of our consciences and conversations, where do they go, all those hard, hurt feelings?

For some of us the pain, the rage, becomes a belt we lash our children with. For others it shrinks down into a tight little knot that we come to call our heart. For others still, for me, the rage went inside and became a fist I beat myself with and beat myself with until I was sure that I was nearly worthless. I was sure of it.

And I suspect sometimes that I would have kept being sure of it had it not been for my daughter, my baby, who was just as sure of the completely opposite point of view and told me so with words, but mostly told me so with her life, her full, incredible, indefatigable engagement with life. It was everywhere and every minute, Nisa's engagement with life and love, and finally I could not ignore and I could not deny it. So, yes, yes it was incredibly hard losing so much so quickly: my marriage, the dream of a shared future. But it has also been incredibly wonderful, perfect even, being this child's mother. Which ultimately is why I am writing this book, and why I am writing it specifically as a single mother. I'm writing to say that for all of the challenges, the children really do make it all worth it. And I'm writing to say that I know I am not the only woman to discover that I can look depression in the face and not call it by another name. I can face it, fight it, and finally, I can—and I am—moving past it. But I am also writing to say that this is no simple proposition, not in the slightest, and so this is how it was at times and this is why it was at times, but finally this was the way out. There was a way out.

AFTER NISA WAS BORN, people asked about her father, where he was, if he had a relationship with his daughter. "It's complicated," I would say at first, and then later, depending on the person, I would take a long, full breath and tell them how it was. I would tell them that Nisa meets her father in the place I met her father, the place I have always met her father. It's a place behind that's hidden, that's behind mountains and then more mountains, behind walls and then more walls. I meet him—we meet him—in a place that is beyond what's familiar, beyond what's comprehensible and perhaps even human. That's where we go, I say: a place beyond peace, but once there, we feel something like peace, maybe even something like beautiful.

Besides, I explain, for us, there is no choice. Despite our prayers, our deep magic, our spells, our potions, and all of our tears, we end up here each time. Here where it is barren, dry, bleak, rotting. Here at the prison. Here where my husband lives, where my child was conceived. Here where she learned the curve of his arm, the nuzzle of his beard. Here where I once did. Here in a prison.

Even in the brightest space of summer, when the sun has pushed aside clouds and everything is gray, the prison sinks in the center from the weight of its austerity. Still, Rashid and I had always refused to be broken by our own reality, a reality that has stretched across years. Undaunted, we proclaimed: We will never be broken by this.

We told each other stories about how we could always work together, a couple, a team, to cast aside that which did not sustain us. And when we could not piece together those stories, we figured out how we could at least make them minor factors, irritations, but not defining. Not of us.

What defined us was the truth in the beauty Rashid and I created, alone, together. Even in that ugly space we arched toward one another and in that space and in that time, no matter what else existed that could break us into pieces, we were whole. This is how we made a child. From that whole place. We owned love and we made love and when that happened, we made love as a complete thing, a sacred thing: love not as a simple act or as simply an act. But love as symphonic, or love as a people's movement, a groundswell, and always love as a state of being, of presence, of grace.

We were able to do this because we were committed to a real world, a living world, not the bizarre matrix of the prison system. It was one too many people knew. It was one that trapped too many, stagnated too many, hurt too many. Rashid and I tried to envision a livable place, one that was meant for real and human habitation. In the world we envisioned, a world where making love was a universe, a grand space that began with a word, a kind expression, a nod or a phrase, a touch or a gesture that said, I understand you and I will not judge you. There was a way in our world to return to joy, a way to achieve touching without fear, without recrimination, without violence, without larceny, without lies. Touching in order to give, never to take.

No matter what family, friends, and others thought and no matter all the doubts those closest to me expressed when I shared with them the reality of my love, my life, they finally agreed that mine was a good life even as my landscape was bordered by the desolate. I remember my little sister, Anne, said that to me once, how despite it all, my life was so blessed. And it was, which is why from that good life, that blessed life, from that stark place, that uninviting place, we made a baby.

We made a shining girl with eyes and hope wider than the sky, wider than even the love that had created her, and this is her story really. Because in the end, she is bigger than us, Nisa is. She is bigger than anything her father and I knew. She is bigger than even the best of our dreams, the best of our love. But I have to tell the story, where it began, how it began. I have to keep on telling it for her so that she knows she came from somewhere beautiful even if the beauty was not laid bare for the world to see. I have to tell it so that she knows why I know, why her father knows how much greater she is than the pieces that made her. I have to tell it so that she knows she was more than a child wanted. She was—she is—a child needed, my Nisa, our Nisa.

Even still I cannot tell it without admitting that no love alone can ever make a human being's journey simple or perfect, and ours has not been, my daughter's or my own. For all of the light, there too has been darkness that seemed completely impenetrable, especially in the very early years of Nisa's life. I am trying to change that. But to make that change means I have to look at it without whimpering or turning away. I have to speak of the failures, my failures, and they track our story. Some of my failures embarrass me in ways I never knew I could feel so embarrassed, ashamed even—and that's a word I hate, a concept I reject.

As a mother I have felt both of these impostures with equal weight. But while my experiences and the personal shame born of them may be particular to me, I know that I am not the only one, not the only mother who has failures stacked up. And yet we are far more than our failures. As alone as I have felt in the years when it seemed as though I had lost nearly everything, the years I am still spending sorting it back out again, sorting myself back out again, at the end of the day what I am certain of is that there are women who have struggled as I have. I want to shake off the hurt now, shake it off of Nisa and shake it off of me and shake it off of all those mothers and children out there, unknown and unnamed, small families, kempt and unkempt, but more often than not, judged, fingers wagged in their faces. I want the hurt off of them.

Which is not to abrogate any single mother's responsibility, surely it's not to abrogate mine. There are times I have to force myself to remember to breathe when I think of all my mistakes, my slips of judgment, and the way they have tracked me and my baby like some madman stalker all the way through, not just moments, but years that I would recall if I could, years for which I would beg, Can I have a do-over? I would beg because how can a mother not beg to erase anything ugly, anything wrong that entered the life of her child?

Of course, we do not get do-overs, much as we would want them. What we get are second chances at best, but second chances are not do-overs. Second chances do not erase your first pass, your first actions. Not if you are a parent. Still, they do have their place. I am only coming to understand that now, the full meaning behind the cliché: Get back on the horse.

But when I am being my most courageous, and when I have gathered up everything I can call on inside of me that is strong and honest, I determine that I will speak of and acknowledge, along with the beauty, every single error, every single misstep. To lie about it, to deny it, only risks its repetition. And we have not always done this, as parents, as adults, even as poet Audre Lorde admonished us two decades ago: "Our silences will come to testify against us out of the mouths of our children." Rather than that, I want to choose truth and reconciliation, even when it is hard, even when it mortifies me.

Because what is also true is that within those times—and I do mean the worst of them—after I became a mother, only after I had this girl—this out-of-my-dreams child, standing or sitting or lying there—an energy, a force reminded me that we would see the other side, we would be in another place. But we really do, as they say, make the road by walking it, by traversing our own course, and no matter how hard it has been at times, this is our course and we will make it by walking together, and when we do, we will understand all the steps we took, all the steps I took. One day even my bad choices will make sense and we will claim the whole of ourselves and the life we have shared. We will be survivors. We will be more than that.

Nisa and I are not all the way on the other side yet, not as free as I want or need us to be. But we are closer to what feels like freedom than we have ever been before and I was not always sure I would be able to say that. With the singular exception of the fact that I had loved deeply in my life and had been loved deeply in my life and from that love I became a mother and being a mother was nearly the total of everything I wanted, I was not sure, for a long time, of much of anything being good or beautiful or safe at all.

WHEN SHE IS OLD enough to understand any part of it, I tell Nisa a story about a girl who was me who was once twenty-three years old. It has felt uncomfortable at times, but I know that what most of us want is to know and understand our root, our core. And we want to think it was good, where we came from, how we got here, that we weren't in error, that our history was not in error. We are living in a time when shame and punishment and one strike you're out is more the norm than not, and this must be especially true for my daughter, for any daughter or son who begins life as the child of a prisoner. She needed to know she was not wrong, wrong is not her name.

"How did you meet Daddy?" she asks, the undercurrent being, Tell me something good, Mommy. Tell me I come from someplace good. In language set to an age and tone that makes sense to her, I tell her once I was twenty-three. I was newly divorced, fully devastated, and without a direction or desire. My first husband, good-hearted and kind, did not wind up being a person with whom I shared similar passions, and before our marriage really began, we'd devolved into a silence that swelled so large it stole all the air and then it was over, our marriage. As they go, we had what some would call a good divorce; no one did anything that could not be forgiven. We love each other even now, but separation still burns you, still leaves you shaky, and I was. I was shaking and looking for something, for someone who would steady me.

"Mommy was trying to figure out what to do with my life," I tell her. "And Mommy loves love," I say. And I tell her how loving love and wanting love, my heart was open when it showed up in the person of a twenty-eight-year-old man named Rashid. Her daddy, I explain as Nisa listens intently, was brimming with ideas and opinions and an impossible optimism. He had completed his degree in sociology, was desperate to enter a master's program. He read books and magazines and articles and scripture as though each chance to read was his last chance to read. "Your daddy is so smart," I tell her, "just like you."

I tell Nisa how I was still in college then. I was an on-again, off-again student, a habitual dropout, but for the moment, right then when I met her father, fully engaged in the academy, a student of political science and Black history.

This is how we met.

As part of my degree requirements, I studied the criminal justice system, in particular its impact on communities of color. The course requirements dictated that we visit a prison, and one Saturday afternoon our professor took several of us up to a facility to sit and talk with men who had committed all manner of crimes—armed robbery, murder. He asked us to try to uncover who they were, who they were beyond their convictions.

"These men come from most of your communities, and have had access or lack of access to the same things you have," our professor reminded us. "Why are you in college," he asked us, "but they're in prison? What choices did you make, what choices did they make, and why? Do we make choices because we have complete free will, or are there other factors, whether we're conscious of them or not, which guide our decision-making process?"

These were questions that would reverberate in my head for years and years to come. At that time, I had no process for making decisions, none beyond the beat of my own heart, a place spilling over with emotions that translated into poems that translated into a longing for real romance, real love. I stood before crowds and said as much in poems I shared because I was certain that what resided inside the muscle that guided the poems could perhaps be a salve, could be a force that could conjure a great, wide, and wonderful life if only I and just one other were willing to embrace it.

And I was willing, which is why when the life of love and romance showed up, even as it did inside a place that pulsed with death, I did not question it. I did not question Rashid, not to the extent one might have expected. Rashid, the man, the student, Rashid the optimist, was also a prisoner, and while in the eyes of many that could be his only title, it never was for me.

Nine years before I met Rashid, he had been sentenced to twenty years to life for his role in a gangland type of murder. He had been a member of a small group of men who shot and killed a man who the group believed was stealing from them.

When I met Rashid, I did not know this. I knew only that he was bright, handsome, always seeking ways to educate himself, ways to transform. We became friends, not just Rashid and I, but all of my classmates who traveled up to that prison with me that first time and all those times after. They, like me, were moved by these men whom society would have us throw away. But our little group believed that no one was disposable, and so they, like me, read poems and had long discussions about the future with the men who were there. And we came to care for some of the men we met and spoke with. And we came to care for Rashid. In this way, he became part of our little clique. Which is why we kept going, why we kept having those talks, reading our poems.

Poetry and words can transform a soul, a person. I believed that then and I believe it now. They had done so for me and I was watching them do so for Rashid, who already had a voracious reading appetite. The longer I knew Rashid, the more I believed in him, and then one day, about a year after we'd met, he called me.

I had given Rashid my phone number after one of the poets in our group read a poem aloud that provoked the guards and we were put out of the prison. I told Rashid to call me when he could so that I knew he and all the other men did not get in trouble for any of our actions. A week, maybe two weeks later, he rang me and said that, no there had been no more problems with the guards, but yes he was reaching out anyway because he wanted me to come visit him. And he was very specific. He did not want to see me as a volunteer or as a poet, but as a friend. I hesitated. I said no. I rebuffed the request several times over. But finally I gave in. The truth was, I liked him.

The first time I visited Rashid in a personal rather than a professional capacity, it was the day after Christmas. This was when he told me everything about his crime. He brought down the transcripts and he encouraged me to read them carefully. He wanted me to know who he had been so I could trust who he had become, who he was still trying to become.

He spoke to me of his shame, and he spoke to me of his desire to do better, to be better. He showed me pictures of his son, born when Rashid was eighteen years old and, as it turned out, would be headed to prison less than two months later. At the end of the visit, we kissed, perhaps a little awkwardly, but certainly intimately. It was a kiss that began a romance.

For five years we courted. We wrote letters, two and three times a week. We spoke on the phone weekly at first, but later, daily. We did our best to shed our fears about vulnerability and trust, and as much as two people can do this, we revealed ourselves to ourselves wholly and without arrogance.

Rashid would be the first person with whom I discussed in depth the molestations that punctured my childhood, that sent me reeling headlong into the world as a girl who by twelve, had no sense of my own youth, and certainly no sense of my own value.

I told him that despite the privileged and in some ways rarefied life that my parents, academics both of them, provided my sister and me, childhood was dangerous. Home for me had been a safe place, but out in the world of schoolteachers, camp counselors, and after-school jobs, danger was a dark cloud that seemed never to lift, never to blow away. And I had ne'er a skill to blow them away myself.

Because I grew up in the years before sexual abuse was discussed openly—or at all—I did not understand even basic things. I did not understand, for example, that the thirty-something-year-old man who claimed me as "his girl" when I was fourteen was a predator. I did not understand anything that happened to me any of the times they happened. I only knew that I felt dirty, wrong, and misplaced in the world.

Rashid encouraged me to seek counseling and supported me when I did. He read books about survivors of sexual violence, and he read books about the partners of survivors of sexual violence so that he could better understand the way I moved in the world, the fears that kept me internally bound. But more than anything else, Rashid listened to me. He refused to minimize my hurt or make judgments about the choices I had made as a girl who had fashioned a life based on hurt. Rashid held me close in every meaningful way a person can hold a person close. I tried to hold him in the very same way. I tried to understand what his life had been.

He told me that he had been a boy who had been abandoned in Guyana. His mother left for the United States when he was an infant, and his father followed some eleven years later. Rashid and his brother, who was a year older, were, for all intents and purposes, left alone to raise themselves during the critical years between twelve and sixteen. And even once he arrived in this new nation, his mother was simply not equipped to parent the child she had left as an infant with an angry and frustrated father who beat his son so badly that at ten years old, Rashid tried to commit suicide.

"I swallowed turpentine," he admitted to me during one

painful visit, even as he added that beating children with canes until they bled was the norm in the world where he grew up.

"No one, including my father, probably including me, would have understood this is abuse. It was the way things were. But still, I was tired of hurting so much."

After months of intense discussions, we fell deeply in love.

For me it was incredible, the very definition of love, because we loved without distraction. All the other loves of my life were fueled and supported by myriad—and sporadic—intimacy: walks in the park, sex, laughter over a dinner, trips to faraway lands.

Rashid and I had none of these experiences to drive our desire or love or relationship. We only had ourselves, our hearts on the table. What other love, I said to him once, could be more pure? After five years of our self-made, self-powered intimacy, we did what most who are in love are wont—and able—to do. We got married. In a corner of a prison visiting room, as vending machines provided the background noise, we exchanged our vows, and then I went home and then he went back to his cell.

An interminable five months after we were married, we qualified for conjugal visits, or trailers, in jailhouse vernacular. Eventually the prison issued us a date, a private forty-four hours together in a small two-bedroom trailer in a yard on the prison compound. The trailers themselves were sparse in their furnishings, funded as they were by the limited monies prisoners cobbled together. But they were clean and they were neat and for those hours, they were home.

I was nervous that first time, afraid even. How do you rise up and meet the years of fantasy we had created about what it

would be like the first time we were together? But in the end, all
that talk, all those years, all that friendship, superseded my hesi-
tations and we made love, again and again. No place was off-
limits. We made love in the bathroom, on the sheets I bought
just for the occasion, in the bedroom, in the kitchenette while I
was trying to make coffee.

But more than that, so much more, we had a period of semi-
normalcy. We made curried chicken and roti together. We
danced slowly to Al Green and Bob Marley. We watched the
news together, we showered together. And yes, at times during
that first visit—and others that followed it—we cried together.

Even now, a decade later, I remember our first trailer visit as
though we had recorded it, as though I had watched a videotape
every night thereafter, meticulously memorizing each movement, each pause, each laugh, all the things we talked about, all
the things we didn't—like birth control and what we would do
if I became pregnant.

Had we discussed it back then, I would have told Rashid that
I would never have a baby with him while he was locked up.
I knew many, many other women with incarcerated husbands
chose to do so, and while I did not disparage their decisions, I
was sure it wasn't for me. As much as I wanted a child, and I
desperately did, I could not see being a single parent. My own
mother and father, married for decades, for decades working
together as a team, working together in love, left me no tem-
plate for a household that did not include two functioning and
healthy adults.

And more, I certainly could not imagine bringing a baby into
a prison. I may have made the choice to enter prisons weekly

for myself, but I was all the way grown, willingly taking on the emotional slop that loving a person who is imprisoned can create. A child was an innocent, unable to weigh both sides of the equation. I could not do it to a baby.

But on that final weekend in September of 1995, I hadn't made such grand pronouncements to Rashid because I didn't believe then that I could get pregnant. I had had so much sex in my life. I had twice lived with men. I had been married once before and yet I had never gotten pregnant. I assumed it was impossible. I went up to the facility and made love with and to my husband and I did not worry.

Three weeks later I discovered I was pregnant.

I never considered keeping the baby. Even as I wept, rubbed my abdomen, claimed my child, listened to Rashid's pleading that I not have an abortion, I never once really considered carrying that baby to term. How could I? It wasn't just the prison or my unwillingness to be a single parent. It was also financial. I wasn't working. I was living in a room in someone else's home, barely eking out an income as a writer and poet.

I had just returned to school to finally finish my bachelor's degree. What did I have to offer a child, save for anxiety and instability? Any child I raised, I told Rashid this, would have everything he or she needed to make it into adulthood safely and sanely.

Still, we argued bitterly—something we'd never really done before—about the decision, but all he could offer me were religious platitudes about life being sacred. But if life was sacred, I would argue back, shouldn't every life be honored with all that it needs, all it deserves? And besides, what about my life? Was my life sacred? I didn't need commandments, I said to my husband. "I need cash. I needed physical support," I told Rashid.

Against my husband's wishes and against the love I felt for that baby who had barely begun to take shape inside of me, and against the desperate need inside of me to be a mother, on a cold Thursday in November of 1995, I had an abortion. In a clinic that felt less like a medical facility than it did a factory, I sat in a hard plastic chair with rows and rows of other women, some far younger than I, some shockingly older. When my name was finally called and I had dispensed with the routine tests—blood work and such—I was led into an ice-cold room where the procedure would take place.

Despite the two doctors and the two nurses who were there, and despite all those women waiting just outside for their turn on the table, it may have been the most alone I have ever felt in my life. I withered into hysteria, crying so hard that the anesthesiologist worried my breathing would be impaired. Later I realized that I probably should have been sent home that day and told to think my decision through some more. But that didn't happen and fifteen minutes later I woke up in the recovery area no longer pregnant.

Regardless of my resolve, my choice to have an abortion—something I knew was absolutely the right thing to do at that time in my life—it caused me guilt and pain for years. Terminating my pregnancy—I felt this then and I feel it now—was against the natural order of things. Had Rashid not been in prison and had we been married under "normal" circumstances, I surely would have had my baby. Or, if we lived a "normal life," if Rashid was home and we discovered we were pregnant but things were such that we did not have the financial wherewithal to begin a family, at the very least I would have done much greater soul-searching before choosing termination. The choice, in other words, would not have seemed so obvious.

But I knew, lying on that examination table in November of 1995, that no matter what the difficulty, I could not go through an abortion with my husband again. The weight of destroying something that was created from a place of great love, destroying something that was part of me, part of us, was unbearable. I carried the weight once. To do it a second time would, literally, destroy me. I told Rashid this. In those raw, ragged days following the procedure, I promised Rashid that if I ever, ever became pregnant again, even if he was still in prison, I would have the baby.

Four years later, in 1999, I would have to stand by those words.

In July of that 1999 I was in the midst of a book tour when Rashid and I were issued a date for a trailer visit. In California at the time, I booked a flight, flew right home, and went immediately into the routine. I packed everything we would need— food, sheets, towels, juice. And, yes, birth control. I wanted to remain careful, as I had since the abortion, although it was less than a week before my period was due. But in truth, I had no fears or even thoughts about pregnancy. I was pretty much thinking only about me, about my career, and what was next up on my literary horizon.

Together in that sterile trailer we'd learned to call home, Rashid and I talked about my dreams. We talked about his dreams, the work he wanted to one day do with young people who were at risk. We talked, as we always did, about life on the outside, life together, and we made love and celebrated the book and we made love some more, and when it was over we parted, sad, but unbroken.

A week later, when my period was a couple of days late, it didn't even occur to me that I might be pregnant. When I noticed I was carrying extra water weight, I blamed it on my nonfunctioning thyroid and intensified my routine at the gym. But after another six or seven days had gone by, I decided, reluctantly, to buy a test. Fast as I could pee on a stick, the thing was turning into dark pink double lines that could not be misread or denied. When Rashid called the next day, I told him directly.

We're having a baby, I said.

Unlike our first pregnancy, I never thought not to have this baby. First of all, that she could create herself in spite of spermicides and a low-probability ovulation moment indicated to me that her presence was beyond any choice I had to make. And then too, I was getting older; I was thirty-two years old when Nisa was conceived. Perhaps I would not have another chance to be the one thing I knew I always wanted to be: a mother. Still, there were fears.

Some were evident. I was an author and freelance writer when I became pregnant. Would I find a real job, decent child care, and be able to survive the predicted sleep deprivation alone? For that matter, would I be able to go through labor without my husband? And though I knew it was ultimately self-defeating, I worried a lot about what people would think. As the child of parents who have been married now for over fifty years, what did I look like, appearing as I did, a single mother?

So okay, yes, being a Black woman factored into the image piece: I mean, did I look like some kind of statistic walking around pregnant with no man in sight? The excoriation of primarily single mothers of color—from the mean-spirited Reaganite notion of the welfare queen, to the pop-culture/hip-hop redaction of women into bitches, golddiggas, and baby mamas—haunted me. They pursued me like angry spirits, hissing through too many of the days, too many of the nights of my pregnancy.

What the world thought of me mattered, perhaps more than it should have. But it did and I wanted it known that I was loved and I was claimed, and that my child was too. I didn't want to be viewed as a woman somebody just got some ass from and then left. I didn't want my child to be seen as a person whose father could leave her. After all those experiences, those real, lived experiences of not being chosen by a man except when I was chosen for violence, yes, I wanted it known that I could be chosen for something more. I was worth something more. I was worth being loved. And more, my baby was too.

Walking these New York City streets alone, I wanted a T-shirt, a placard, anything that would declare to the world once and for all that I was not the discarded woman, perhaps the hated woman, the bad girl, the nasty girl, the girl who could be fucked, impregnated, tossed aside, and dismissed. And then there were the larger political concerns, the ones beyond my own personal demons.

For as long as I have been conscious of it, I have done what I could to refuse at every turn slipping on a jacket some racist or misogynist had sewn.

But in what real way could I fight back against my fears, the ones inside of me, the ones looming everywhere outside? My attempts were, at best, pathetic: painfully, with the aid of lotion, water, and soap, I squeezed my wedding rings onto my fingers long after they had swollen into things that looked more like fat little sausages. In doctors' offices and later at the midwifery center where I gave birth, I looked at no one, sat up proudly, made calls on my cell phone to girlfriends, figuring Rashid or "my husband," as I proclaimed a little too loudly, into the conversation. When the time came, I paid for private birthing classes so I would not have to sit with other women as their loving partners caressed their bellies.

But I worried most of all, though, about protection. Would I be able to raise a Black girl safely in a world that seems only to expand in its ability to hate and destroy? In a culture whose practices—from health care to policing—tip toward death, with Black people and women more often than not the stand-ins for the bull's-eye, would the life of one Black girl be honored by anyone other than me?

Would my love and honor for her be enough to sustain her through to maturity? The constant reports of drug and alcohol abuse among young people; the sexual and physical violence that has become integrated into pop culture as though it's a sexy god-damn courting ritual; the girls who at eight years old are giving blowjobs to boys in the schoolhouse stairwells and coming home with STDs in their mouths; and the seeming tidal wave of so-called good girls out on the stroll in Brooklyn, Atlanta, and the suburbs, simply put, scared the shit out of me.

Not because I judged or disliked any of these kids, but

because I'd been my own '80s version of them. I knew how that slippery slope could be a challenge to circumvent. Would my little girl be able to do what I could not?

When my child reached an age when she too would have to negotiate streets and sex and perhaps even simple fucking survival, would she know how to speak to me, as I did not know how to speak to my parents? Would I know how to listen to her, hear what she was telling me, read between her lines? My parents, in all of their brilliance and commitment, were unable to do that for me. During my adolescence, teenage angst became the nomenclature for what eventually revealed itself as a clinical depression that at its worst spiraled down into suicidal ideation.

It would be years, so many, before I could name the hurt, try to heal it. Would I repeat a vile pattern with my daughter? After all, I had both of my parents present, loving me. My daughter only had me. These questions, more than the physical challenges of pregnancy, kept me awake through the nights, staring at everything and nothing, and wondering, worrying, where could I go, where could I live and raise my child safely?

In 2000, the year my daughter was born, the nightly news reported that the only presidential campaign that was deeply rooted in the reclamation of family values was the one that was also headed up by a man who had signed 153 death warrants during his turn as governor.

I wanted to run, go live off the grid, have my child, tell no one, or keep her forever in my womb.

But the more round my tummy became, the more my breasts swelled, the more these fears either fell away or shrank into something I could manage. I gave myself over to reason, faith, hope, and Dr. Spock. I left the shaky financial world of freelance and accepted a job as an editor at a women's magazine. I made it through labor, according to many, quite easily; although Nisa came two weeks late, when my water did break at exactly 12:01 AM on April 14, 2000, less than eleven hours later my daughter was in my arms, having already learned to latch on. Seven hours after that, we were home entertaining people, eating gourmet take-out pizza.

And it all seemed so possible, right then, that night, surrounded by friends and food, the love of my husband, my daughter's father, palpable, however distant; we felt him there and said it, everyone did.

Rashid called and checked in on us daily, and I updated him with breast-feeding reports, how many diaper changes, who'd come by to see the baby, how much she'd slept—or in Nisa's case, did not sleep. I begrudgingly admitted that she did look a bit like him, though I tempered that with an admonishment. "Why should you get any credit? You just showed up for the party. I did all the work," I said and laughed and Rashid laughed too.

We laughed so much in those first days. We laughed and we spoke bravely about Rashid's parole date, which was just under three years away. Given all the people we'd seen the parole board turn loose, even as everyone knew they were still dangerous, we felt a sense of confidence. Again and again, we would go over all of Rashid's accomplishments in prison, the master's in theology, his superclean record, the people, including some cops, who supported his release, and we declared that there was no way they wouldn't let him out, especially now with this beautiful girl in the picture. We planned it all out, from Rashid's first day home to all the days after, the days, he would say, with a threatening grin, when he would "put a whole bunch more babies in you, girl."

We saw a future, our future, defined more by the mundane than the misfortuned.

We talked about backyards, family vacations, running errands together, about Rashid driving me to work, picking me up. We talked and we planned and it was not particularly fancy and it was not particularly nuanced nor was it particularly sparkling. But it was simple and it was clear and it was ours, and from the day Nisa was born, I offered it up, that vision of the future, to my daughter, as though it were true, as though our dreams were prophecy.

Long before spoken language was the most effective method of communication between us, I whispered to Nisa about the man I loved, my husband, her father, how now he was away from us but it would not always be so. I issued out return-of-the-father dates to Nisa, to myself, and called these dates hard dates, called these dates facts.

I did not foresee that all the facts were lies.

The stories in my head, the ones I had written about a great love that grew in the dark, the stories I was writing, just then, abundant with new life, about the homecoming, the love finally allowed into the light—these stories did not allow me the gift of foresight or even objective reasoning. They only allowed me hope and when hope is all you have to feed your great hunger, you can chew on it and chew on it, but hope alone cannot sustain a body or create a new day.

It's only now, eight years on, eight years a mother, eight years spiraling, and eight years removed from the story I always thought I would tell—the one with the neatly packaged happy ending and the one Rashid and I will never be able to write—that I can begin to tell the story as it really was. It can take a lifetime to face the truth or it can take eight years. But no matter how long, it's still going to be there, the truth, even if at its frayed center is you and your baby. And even if the fraying, the fractures, the flaws, are as much your fault as they are anyone or anything else's. You have to face it, the truth, quietly or loud, publicly or privately, or some measure in between. It's not going anywhere.

Because as much as I could love a good, long lie about my life and my choices, I know the back draft. We've all seen it in families, maybe even our own, where lies ruled the day. Secrets and lies give way to everything from broken relationships to cancer to alcoholism.

So now the stories I tell are different than the ones I once did. I've learned to be much more careful in what I say and how I say it. All those whispers in her ear promising when her daddy would be home and what life would be—and then what life became—taught me the fallibility of my once-upon-a-time quixotic stories. I know better now the difference between those stories that save and those that just sit there, pretty perhaps, but ultimately useless. And I know this too: between those two kinds of stories is the immeasurable space that exists between romance and love, nostalgia and history. Fiction and nonfiction.

Thankfully, Nisa and I also know the power of the real stories, the power of the truth—that particular honesty, that particular truth that mothers owe their daughters. Told correctly, those stories give the teller and listener both the power to reinvent what is in front of them and the inspiration and audacity to remix the elements until they're something that can nourish, something that is real. That is the muscle, the sinew of real stories, hard as they may sometimes very well be.

Every story of every life has its own beginning. That we are ever able to properly locate it is, for me, the enduring question. But as best as I can locate it, what I've shared with you is our beginning, Nisa's and my own. And our beginning—the one that, yes, harks back to the meanest of places—is, in the face of it all, still brimming with a love and with a vision so grand we believe in it. More than anything else, we believe in us.

We believe in our own two hands and our own two hearts. We believe in our minds and our spirits and our muscle and our breath. We believe in the strength that we can call on together, one mother, one daughter, standing and pushing and dreaming and creating with the determination and force of laborers, those wizards whose magical and hard, hard work can turn sand and stone into pyramids and prisons into particles.

statistics don't tell the story.
the story tells the story.

I have to make an admission, one that may put so much that comes later—my terrible sadness, I mean—into context. But it is also the one that also sounds completely insane, given the specifics of my life, my situation, my own lived experiences. Anyway though, here it is, the truth, the thing that I believed down to the core of me: I never imagined I would be a single mother.

When I say never, I mean never. I mean not once during my pregnancy. Not once during all those times I was huge and pregnant and I wanted someone to make my tea and no one was there, or even when I worried about how people saw me at doctors' offices, waddling and alone. I did not see myself as a single mom then or even when I was the only one waking up at 2:30 AM, at 5:30, to feed my baby.

Various reports tell us that there are a growing number of women who choose to single-handedly have a child, a coparent being either unavailable or else not of interest. If these reports are true, I certainly respect their choice. But it was not mine, nor was it the decision of scores of other sisters who wake up one day suddenly alone, their partners having been put out or else having slipped out, to be with another person, to be alone, or to be, for whatever reasons, just someplace else. For most of us, I suspect, single parenting is less a choice than a place we end up.

A few months into Nisa's life, when things came undone for me, for our family, I spent a great deal of time being jealous of this woman I knew. Despite the outward courtesy I extended to her, I don't believe I harbored even one kind thought about her then. And when I could, I lobbed any petty remark at her. I was really trifling.

I would look at her and think how she seemed to have it all: a great job; what appeared to be extraordinary respect from her peers; a gorgeous husband and beautiful baby; a stunning house—a home she owned, unlike me, still a renter in a city fast closing out those of us unable to scrounge up the money to make a six-figure deposit on a seven-figure home, because that's what homes can cost here in New York, even in some of the most dilapidated of neighborhoods.

But the point is, I wanted her life to be my life. I thought that each time I saw her. I wanted what appeared to be the neatness of her life, the prettiness of it. I wanted the fancy borders and silk curtains of her life. I wanted the no prisons of it. I wanted anything, anything, anything that would move me away from being considered by anyone as strange or pathological, off-center or incapable as a parent.

And then one day—or this is how it seemed from the out-side looking in—one day it all ended for her, just like that. The husband was gone, the house was gone, the job was gone. What had been so beautiful before, if it really was beautiful before, now seemed especially cruel.

She had known the top of the mountain, so to speak. She had

known a place I had never even seen and so had no true idea of what I was missing. But to know it, to have touched it, and then to have it taken, snatched up and away! And it was a while before she said it, before she claimed her space, this new space. In the beginning, just after the sudden split, she saw in the husband she was now separated from, a coparent and said so.

Specifically she said, "asha, I understand the details of your life, but mine are very different. I am not a single mother like you are."

And I realized that I used to believe things like this, even if not say them, to all the sisters I knew from the prisons. I started considering again all those mothers I would see each week waiting for a bus or van or on a line in the rain waiting to get into a correctional facility, child in hand. When I first became a mother, I believed arrogantly that those among the group who identified themselves as single parents claimed that term because their man wasn't as good as mine. Their man must not have supported them the way Rashid supported me. I was a married woman and felt every part of being married. I was not a single mother. Not like them. That's what I thought. I thought it just as that sister with the disappearing man thought it about me. Both of us were wrong.

Inevitably, she would come to know what I would come to know. She would, of necessity, modify herself as I modified myself. It happened a few months on, when the responsibility of child rearing had firmly planted itself in the corner of her checkbook, her social life, her sex life and work life, in her corner but not her ex-husband's corner. Then she would say something else. But at first, there was disbelief, rejection.

I completely understood.

I do not care that it is prevalent. Raising a child alone should not be asked of any one person. Even two parents is far too small a number, far fewer than what it really takes to nudge or nurture or sometimes shove a child up through to maturity. We do it, of course, on our own. And many do it exceedingly well. But that's not the point.

Parenting is all about replaying David and Goliath. It's about having to go toe-to-toe against entities immeasurably larger than you are or ever will be: from the fast-food chains to the soft-porn music videos pumped out newer and nastier each passing minute, from Christmas and Halloween and all the other holidays that celebrate nothing but how much money one mom, one dad, one family, can spend.

You fight the health-care system, the educational system, everything out there that would make a one-size-fits-all solution for your very individual child and his or her very individual needs. If you don't have the wherewithal to gangsta up when the time comes, Goliath will win.

He will win and then head off to fight his next David, and your loss, your baby's loss, will be forgotten just that quick. I don't know if it is by instinct, but I do know that at some point, most mothers get this, which is why it happens, why a woman might go into shock and denial when she wakes up one day and realizes, wow, this is all on me. I think that this is what happened to the woman I knew. This is what happened, at least in part, to me.

Initially, though, I thought of Rashid as away, but not gone. Rashid was a coparent, albeit a parent forced to live far away, like a man whose work kept him in a distant city. But I never thought of my husband as an absentee father; the first year of Nisa's life, Rashid sent me money every month for our daughter. He sent money until his funds were depleted. And while cash cannot replace real human presence, I felt supported. I thought I could hold out across the hard first years, the lonely ones. I thought that was all I would have to do.

Rashid was going to come up for parole for the first time before Nisa turned three. That was a given. All of the appeals had been exhausted and we no longer crossed our fingers and toes, hoping for a movielike ending: Rashid, triumphing over the courts and sweeping into our lives at just the critical moment. We let that fantasy go. But if all went well, and neither of us had any reason to believe things would not go well, the less dramatic outcome would surely come to pass: Rashid would make parole and be home to help me plan and then to celebrate Nisa's third year of life.

As my body swelled, Rashid and I had swooned over sonogram photos in the prison visiting room, and weekly we discussed our future in what appeared to be rational rather than fantastical terms, which, if we are honest, is what we had done for all those years when we believed a court reversal would free Rashid and send him home to me—now me and Nisa—before he had served out every day of his twenty-year sentence.

We were different now, things were different now. Now there was a baby in the mix. And now we had an obligation to face reality. Which is not to say that before Nisa we were completely lost in fantasy. But now there were diapers to change, clothes to be bought, doctors to be seen, child care to find. There was a real live and tiny person who could not speak for herself.

We had to speak and think for her in ways we never did for ourselves, because there is nothing more real than a hungry or sleepy or wet child crying.

Rashid and I spoke then in very confident and definite terms about his preparation for parole. Unlike the appeals process, which can be capricious—judges do not like to overturn the decisions of other judges—parole and who is eligible for it has clear guidelines that govern who can and should be considered for release. Are you remorseful? Have you done good time? Have you taken advantage of what the state deemed rehabilitative? Do you have a post-release plan and a post-release support system? Is there anything that indicates that you might be a future danger to society? If it was a test, Rashid would have achieved a perfect score.

"There are a lot of people, asha," Rashid told me one afternoon, "who have agreed to consider supporting my release. But I know they need time to weigh things over, get letters written. All that. That's why I want to start early. So I have a whole real package together by the time I go before the parole board. By then I should be finished with my master's too. So they've got to see I'm not the same kid I was then. I mean, you know?"

"Yup. I know," I agreed. But really, did I? Did he?

He went on to emphasize how important his studies were, the master's program he had just been accepted into at Sing Sing Correctional Facility. "You know brothers who do that program don't come back?"

"What do you mean?"

"I mean the rate of recidivism is so low among those brothers it doesn't even rate. It's like less than one percent."

I shook my head in disbelief and felt assured. How could I not? How could I, how could Rashid, ever have imagined that anything would stand in the way of his release? He'd done what the system had demanded he do. He'd become a person who let the time serve him, as we say, rather than simply just serving the time. This is why I knew he would be granted parole and why I did not think of myself as single. Rather, I thought of myself as I was: married, partnered, and claimed. I was not a woman who had been fucked one hot night and then discarded. I was claimed, me, asha. I was claimed and I was loved. So too was my baby. I felt this with everything that breathed inside of me, felt that with her breathing inside of me.

Even when I went up to the prison, taking Nisa for the first time when she was fifteen days old, and the guards, with their angry, their suspicious eyes, looked over me and looked over my baby and told me the number of bottles and diapers I could bring in—three was the limit on both—I did not think of myself as alone. Or when I argued with the guards, explaining to them that my daughter sometimes drank more than three bottles of milk over the course of six hours, which was the length of the visit, and I knew I was the only person in the whole world who knew just how much milk my hungry little baby drank, what her sleep habits were, what she needed—because no one else was there with us, so no one else knew—but even then I thought of myself as somebody's wife. I never thought of myself as a woman sort of swashbuckling it alone out there against monsters and general ne'er-do-wells, all to secure the life of her child.

Nor did I think it later, when we had been processed into the prison and my hand had been stamped with the invisible ink that identifies me as a visitor rather than a prisoner, and I then had to fight with the guard about how he could not, absolutely not, stamp my daughter's fifteen-day-old hand. Even then, I felt connected.

And I felt it when my breasts filled with milk and Rashid, watching me shift and frown from discomfort, leaned over and whispered in my ear how he longed for the ability to make me comfortable. But I needed to nurse or pump, two realities of motherhood not available on that six-hour visit—it's no surprise that you can't just pull out your breast and let your baby latch on in a prison visiting room. I mean, people frown on that in liberal areas of New York and San Francisco, but as a new mother I wondered how hard would it have been to have a chair in the ladies' room where we could sit with our babies and feed them? But these are issues you don't raise in a prison when your goal is most of all to fly below the radar, thereby avoiding the wrath of guards. Really, you do in prisons what we do in so many other places. Face whatever the situation is, no matter how much you want to shift, no matter how uncomfortable you are.

"I wish I could make this easier for you," he began softly. "I swear I would do anything. I would do anything," he continued as he rose slowly from his seat, stood behind me, rubbed my back, and then his fingers through my hair. And I leaned into him, leaned into his hard stomach, and closed my eyes and felt safe and felt a future.

And then again later, I felt it, the future, as I watched Rashid hold his tiny daughter for the first time and the tears pushed against the corners of his eyes and then they pushed against the corners of my eyes, which was also the moment when I knew,

I knew, I was looking at a man for whom—for all his years of penance and prayer, all of his struggle to transform himself, all of his remorse—this was it, the moment when he understood in every part of his DNA, the complete and total preciousness of life.

And I did too. I understood it even more in the presence of my husband as he held his daughter, our daughter, and we talked about how one day, sooner rather than later, we, Nisa and I, would know *father* as an action word.

"When I come home," he promised, "you'll never have to do anything alone again." I believed him. I can't imagine believing such a thing now. Now, I can't imagine relying on anyone for anything, unless perhaps if I'm paying them. But then it was different and everything possible was so close. "It's right here, baby," Rashid would say. "The end of all this is right here." And he was right, of course. The end was right there. It just wasn't the end we had bargained and planned for. But there was no one to tell us and so no way to know. It's why we were sure all challenges would be mitigated by the love and the promise of a certain tomorrow.

On the day Nisa was with her father for the very first time, we looked at all the pictures I'd sneaked in that were taken of Nisa's birth, and Rashid said, "It almost feels like I was there," and I said, "I felt like you were there." And that lie from my mouth sat there between us, a dead thing, a thing that smelled bad, but we did not notice right then. We did not notice it because we did not know it was a lie.

We only knew our dreams, our push for an ever brighter tomorrow, and as we spoke of our tomorrows, Nisa nuzzled herself into Rashid's chest and fell asleep right there, not for long, but long enough for him to take in her baby smell, implant the memory of it someplace that could not be searched or discovered or confiscated or destroyed. I could not have been convinced then, in that visiting room, watching Nisa and her father there and then, that I was single, alone.

Nor did I think of myself as single or as alone later that first afternoon that we three, our family, shared together, when the day slammed shut and the guard was yelling out that visiting hours were over. I thought, It will not always be this way. We are connected, a team, and one day, sooner rather than later, there will be neither guards nor doors to regulate the expression and existence of our family.

Even still it's true that when that visit came to an end, Rashid nearly convulsed, not visibly, and not in any sort of way that another would notice unless you were a person who cared for him enough to really notice him, see him beyond a department number, a conviction. And I did. I loved him enough, I loved us enough, which is why I saw it, that thing inside a man, that piece of spirit that crumples up inside him when he cannot escape a situation that takes away parts of his humanity. They survive this, some do, and come back and grab hold again of themselves and assert their spirits when the time is right. But you and that man both know he will never be the same person again, never go back to a certain place in his heart. That's what I saw at the end of the day I took Nisa to meet her father for the very first time: a man who would now have to forever traverse the world shielding a piece of his spirit and so a man who would, in a sense, never be free.

There was nothing to be said and there was nothing to be done, because sometimes there is just nothing. There is just nothing. Prisons taught me that. But even as I knew there was nothing, no salve, no immediate remedy, I did not feel apart or separate. I did not feel as though I was a single mother. I was part of a team. I was sure of it.

I was sure of it and I said it and we said it. We said it over and over, one hundred times, and then one hundred times more. Then we went about blocking out the crippling features of the life we were living, focusing instead on anything that made us feel attached to a life that didn't have barbed wire wrapped around it. And never once did we prepare ourselves for a life without one another.

Not even just after coming home from that first visit, when I sat beneath the dim orange light of my bedroom and I was holding Nisa, waiting for her father to call us, to check on us, as he always did: "Home safe, baby?" he asked, although obviously we were. And I stared at my baby girl and I wondered how much of this prison life she would retain, how much would recede far back into her memory.

That night I wondered too if there would ever be a voice in her life that recalled one of those terrible, hate-filled guard voices, and if that voice would call her back to a bad place. And yes, of course, I wondered what choice I had made, what I had done to an innocent child. Yet even then, cloaked—not so much cloaked, but bound by my own hopes and dreams, even then I did not feel alone.

From that first visit and on visits that came after, Rashid and I made plans. We talked about finances, child care, and how long

I should breast-feed. We talked about religious instruction, how we would restrict television, whether to raise our girl vegetarian, vegan, or meat eating. We committed to serving only organic foods, obviously no pork, but also no beef, though chicken and fish were fine. (In the years since that decision, Nisa has rejected our food restrictions. While there's still no pork in her life, Nisa declared one day recently that although all those animals were really, really cute, she "still had to eat steak and lamb and stuff. It's just so juicy, Mommy!"). And religion? I don't practice but Rashid is still a very pious man. We argued a bit about our daughter's engagement with religion, but I reminded him that he had come to Islam on his very own terms, walked on his own out of Catholicism. "Let Nisa decide for herself," I pushed and he finally agreed. "We won't keep anything from her," I said, "but let her find her own way like you did."

"Okay. Okay," Rashid said, acquiescing one day, adding quietly, truthfully, that "the religion cannot be compelled. But I want her to know who I am."

"She will," I promised, and then we moved on to other areas that would define our baby's life. We mulled over the kind of schools we would want our child to attend, the suburbs or the city, places our daughter should see in the world, how many more babies we wanted to have someday, and whether I should work once Rashid came home. We talked and sometimes we struggled through things. We visited and revisited all sorts of theories about what makes for quality parenting. But we did it together, we did it as a couple. We did it just like any other brand-new mother and father.

family tree

Beyond the weekly sojourns up to the prison, in all of the ways that matter the most, in the same way that Rashid and I discussed the future as any other new parents, so too did Nisa and I live like the majority of new mothers and children. We were completely attached, fascinated by each other. Okay, well, perhaps she wasn't fascinated by me, but I was by her. Still, I beamed when I saw how easily comforted she was by the sound of my voice, the voice that had been speaking to her for nine months in utero, the voice she heard first every morning, last every night.

Even as she was barely weeks old, everything Nisa did seemed to me to be a miracle, a moment to be captured, shared, bragged about, held forever in my heart. Her discovery of her hands, the different faces she began to make, my God, I thought, no other child ever before, no other child ever after. I thought she was a genius and suddenly understood all those other parents I'd met over the years who always had ten or fifteen pictures of their children there at the ready.

Humans will learn more between the time we are born and when we turn five years old, than we will for the rest of our lives.

Nisa's developing brain was taking in more information than I would ever again, even if I lived for another sixty or seventy years. It was a daunting process to witness and often I couldn't imagine how hard it was, the toll it must take on the small-est among us. Early on, there were those who could not believe what they perceived to be my unusual patience with Nisa, but it wasn't so much patience that I had, but reverence. And that reverence was rewarded; Nisa's first word was "happy."

And she was, despite whatever challenges that she did not know were complicating our lives, Nisa was such a happy baby. And watching her discover life invited me to do the same, to see possibility everywhere and embrace it. That is what our begin-ning was, Nisa's and my own, in the living colors of our home, and it was magic and joyful and perfect and if I was ever that blissful before, I don't remember it.

I only know that we were at the edge of summer, the days just before June after a spring in which there had been snow in April. But now it was May and the city was quietly alive in a pastel warmth and we strolled in it, through it, across it.

Years earlier an acquaintance of mine had referred to her two-year-old son as her best friend. She was a single parent and her son was her constant companion in cafés and parks where she went to write or just sip coffee or tea. Back then I thought that she lacked proper boundaries. *How could your child be your best friend?* I wondered but did not say.

Having Nisa taught me that what my friend meant, all those years ago, wasn't that her son was her best friend as in, a steady emotional support, but best friend as in, *there is no one else I would rather be with most of the time.* Not that you have much choice when you're raising a child on your own, but what I know I feel and what I believe she felt was that there was no one else who could bring us more pure joy than our children. I know there's no one else whose laughter gives me such breath and movement. No one.

Of course there are friends with whom I enjoy spending time without my daughter, but when I'm with Nisa, even to this day, it's all brand-new, a fresh journey, and I am all too aware that I will wake up one day and it will be gone, the expanse of time I now get to spend with her. As I write these words in this very moment, Nisa is steadily securing her role as a grammar school star. Her time with me is shrinking. I am no competition now for a sleepover with three or four other girls who are her own age. But for as long as I can have her, for as long as I have a choice in the matter, more often than not, my daughter is my choice when it comes to who I want to be with and experience the world.

But yes, there are people—friends—who have called me smothering. They've shaken their heads at me and warned me against stifling Nisa's independence. Generally I don't argue back, because to explain your parenting style is to then be dismissed as defensive. I've learned to let it go, because it's not important that they know or acknowledge what I'm trying to make happen in Nisa's life. It's only important that Nisa continues to be the loving child she is. I actively work now to shut out voices so loud that they shut me out and shut me down for years and years, but finally I got it, that Nisa is happy and Nisa is thriving and so what else? Motherhood was my choice. It was more than a choice, it was my deepest desire.

There was nothing I wanted more than to be a mother. I had seen much of the world; written two books; known great and defining love. I had certainly been to more than my fair share of parties, more than my fair share of clubs. Motherhood was then and is now exactly where I want to be. To be pregnant with a child that was made with the love of my life, my husband, was a dream come true for me, despite the obvious hard edges of it.

But if I was to be honest, and alone and away from all the criticism that penetrated my parenting style, my lifestyle in general, I knew that my desire for a child was so much larger than having no interest in parties, no interest being in the mix. A mother now, I could begin to look at something I had spent my life both running into and away from. It is the story that is part of my bloodstream, defines it, my genetic twists.

And the thing about it is that it isn't especially obvious, not like a physical deformity or birthmark you can witness and name. Nevertheless it has been both of these to me. But once I became a mother, once I gave birth, I could not stop thinking of it, and I could not avoid it and I could not deny it.

Having been adopted near my third birthday, I had never seen, at least to my memory, one person who looked like me, or shared my blood and particular genetic makeup.

I may never understand why this hurt me so badly, left me feeling for my whole life as though I came from nowhere, belonged to no one. But it has. It always has. And it was there all during my pregnancy. It was there all during the time that I refused to see myself as a single mother. It was there, that thing, that heavy tarplike thing that hung over my head, my heart, and reminded me I was not the one worth being claimed.

I was the one who could always be given away. Nisa would never feel that. She would never know that. She would know that she was wanted, that she was wanted every day of her life. She was wanted before she even got here and she was wanted by her father and she was wanted by me. Me who looked like no one, came from nowhere. I looked at Nisa and was certain that as much as she came from me, I came from her.

One of Rashid's friends—this was during our first visit—stopped by our table and looked at Nisa and said loudly, "Man, that girl's all you, Rashid. All you." He was joking, playing, but those words slapped. He could not have known, that man. But Rashid did. He knew all of my past, and knowing, he rushed to my defense. "That mouth, those eyes, those ears. That's *all* asha. Can't you see, man?" he implored and almost sounded convincing. This is what Rashid knew: I needed Nisa to look like me. I *needed* it.

Nisa may very well have been my present and my future, but in a very real way, she was also my past. She was, to be sure, where I was headed, but her very life said everything about where I had been, who I had been, who I had not been, who I had not come from, where I had not come from. So there it is, perhaps the whole of my story whittled down into a few short paragraphs. And yes, I mean it's also true that, of necessity, I have had to have little faith in blood ties. But I longed for them, longed for what I imagined they carried, all that history, those unbreakable bonds, unbroken.

The oft-repeated interpretation by my parents, the ones who adopted me, the only ones I have ever known, is that I was twice loved—first by my birth mother, who must have wanted the very best of homes for me, which is why she gave me away, and then second, I was loved by them, by my adoptive parents, the ones who chose me. Chose me willingly.

My own take on it, which was evidenced about as well as my parents' version of the truth, was that I was the mistake, the one who could—and would—always be given away. Everywhere inside of me has lived the story of a child who—sight unseen—was unwanted. I admit that that changed, sort of, when the social worker and my adoptive parents—and I do not wish to minimize the only people who have ever taken responsibility for me, and people whom I love deeply—scooped me up nine-one-one-style late one winter night out of a foster home that was rife with trouble that no one, even now, can fully disclose to me.

What I will tell myself like a mantra even to this day is that my parents came to my rescue only because they'd already met me once or twice before at the orphanage or whatever it was. People stepped in—and I realize too that this makes me lucky—because it was apparent that there was something wrong in the foster home I lived in at the time. Even before that night, I am told, my social worker would periodically take me to meet other potential parents. From the beginning, there were concerns.

My mother, father, and I, it is said, got along famously from the very beginning. As their version of the family history goes, I was a very pretty child, startlingly verbal, inquisitive, and affectionate, an all-around charmer. I was two and half years old.

But what if I had not been? What if I had been obviously flawed? I mean, all humans bear flaws, but some of us hide them better and I'm a master at hiding. But this is the question. Would my parents have chosen me? What qualities must a child possess to be chosen, accepted, taken in and loved? And not just children who are adopted, but all of our children? Is there some predetermined formula that makes one kid count and another counted out?

What if I had been shy or a crier, not too bright, maybe a little funny looking? Would I have been relegated to the dank, pest-infested cellar of child rearing: multiple foster and/or group homes? Or would there have come a moment when the new parents, foster or adoptive, grew tired of me, gave me back? If someone whose body you grew inside of could give you away, then anyone could? Right? This the story behind any story I tell the world about who I am.

My story is not about being a charming Black girl who graduated high school at fifteen, rides English, and can discuss opera or hip-hop depending on the audience. My story is about a girl who believes if she is not perfect she will be left behind; it's kind of an ultimate tale of childhood horror about being the last one picked, or worse, the one never picked at all when the kids on the playground are choosing sides.

Here's the point. I wanted a family and most especially a child, a child from my own womb, because I wanted someone who would love me, flaws and all. Because didn't they have to, didn't we have to, well, love each other no matter what? We were, after all, family, *and* we had the damn DNA to prove it.

I know this is not logical. Clearly shared DNA did not make my birth mother bond with me, her baby. And the lack of DNA did not stop my parents from loving me or from raising me. But still I believed it had to count for something, all those stories demonstrating the thickness of blood.

And oh God, I know all this sounds so selfish, as though my daughter is here to live for me and not the other way around. Or more accurately, it sounds as though I don't know we are here in equal measure, living and giving to each other and ourselves as best we can. I do know this.

But I know too that humans are social creatures. We're not crocodilian, content to crouch in the weeds, alone with our own shadows. We want to belong. We need to. We want to be understood by others who are like us, others whom we in return understand. We want a tribe.

Unlike friends of mine who had huge, almost unmanageable biological families and a genealogy that could be traced down through generations—a great-great-grandmother's face that comes back to visit in the eyes, smile, or shape of progeny a century on—I had no such beginnings, no stake in a past, no history, no root. So what other choice did I have really? If I wanted to locate myself, to be part of a continuum, and to be sure, I did want it, I had, then, to create it.

Nisa is my tribe, my family tree, branches and all.

And how do you explain that, how do any of us explain who we are as parents, how we got there, the roads we took, the roads we wish we could have taken, when friends or family begin to swarm, sometimes wag their finger, offer advice about how you can be a better mother. This is what I am trying to explain. You don't do it. It's a game you'll never win. What you do, finally, is summon the courage to look at your own self in your own mirror and value what you can, value as much as you possibly can. Value you yourself as much as you humanly can. And then you hug your baby, and you do everything you can to set aside anyone and anything that does not honor either of you. You get help if you need to, if you can't do it alone. And then you just keep it moving. You keep it moving real, real fast. Maybe that's wrong. But that's what I did. That was, right then, especially in the beginning, all I could do. Even now sometimes, it's all I can do. Just keep moving.

girl child in a compromised land

*Y*ou were not yet two months old on that night when we were curled up together in my room. The news was on and the anchor was reporting mayhem at the annual Puerto Rican Day Parade. There were disturbing reports about women being snatched up, shoved around among the men gathered there.

The women were being groped, they were being groped violently. The police who were at the scene, Nisa, the same ones this society will tell you are there to serve and protect you, were laughing at the girls, who at this point were crying. This was on the news that night, Nisa, the news you could not understand, but I understand it, I do. Me, the mother of a girl child. Me, who was once a girl and who remembers cops like this, cops who laugh at young girls being groped. They did it to your auntie once, laughed when she told the cops that it was that man right there who had hurt her in a store in the section where they kept the Suzy Q's and Twinkies. Your auntie was nine then or maybe she ten. They did it to my high school girlfriend Xiomara, seventeen, whose boyfriend was a cop, thirty-five. His friends laughed at her and she heard them laugh and later told me so in our high school cafeteria. "Got you some nice tight pussy." And now over fifteen years later, what has changed, baby girl of mine?

I am looking at these girls on the six o'clock news, the ones who talked to reporters and filled in the blanks about what had happened earlier that day and I am thinking that they, like you right now, once lay upon their mother's breast. And all their mothers wanted was to protect them. It's what I want most of all. Perhaps their mothers drifted off then, as I do now, into prayer about all the hurt and humiliations they had known. All the hurt and humiliations they were going to fight to ensure their daughters avoided.

It was hard enough to sidestep the indignities and pain when they were secretive, a dirty thing, an accepted wrong. But when the dirty thing, the mean shit, the cruelty, is made mainstream and called fun, what do we do to combat it? How does a mother raise her girl? What weapons does she brandish and teach her daughter to use, what armor? When do I begin her training, her tactical skills? When do I tell her the truth? When do I say, Nisa, they don't love us. And how do I say it, without either being hyperbolic or understated?

You are no longer a baby. This letter is taking years to write. The night we lay together when I watched the news about the parade has long since passed, and yet I still struggle with the very same questions. How do I tell you what's real, what is the way to be safe, to keep you safe, and where do I start? Do I begin in 1993 with Snoop and it ain't no fun if my homies can't get none?

Or was it when Nelly swiped a credit card down White Chocolate's ass?

Do I start with a bitch is a bitch?

Or should I let it all go and get right to the heart of the matter? Maybe I need only mention the girls in the schools in Colorado, Canada, and Pennsylvania who were singled out, lined up, sexually assaulted, and then murdered, murdered? And while every one

*expressed concern about the spate of violence in American schools—
How do we make the classroom secure? policy- and homemakers
demanded— no one, at least no one whose voice was covered by the
news, was asking, what does it mean that there's an epidemic of violence directed against the girls? Who asked, How do we secure our
female children? The ones from Southeast Asia sold into sex slavery
at nine years old; the ones in the Horn of Africa, and then far beyond
that region, whose vaginas are mutilated; the ones down the hall in
the über-expensive co-op in mid-Manhattan with the daddy who
can't keep his dick in his pants when he looks at his daughter. These
were not topics on morning-show discussions. There were no special
broadcasts about violence against women. There was a moment of
outrage against Don Imus and a longer moment against vulgar rap
lyrics, but no time spent examining the thing itself, that which gave
space to an Imus or a gangsta rapper in the first place.*

*Should I ever tell you, Nisa, about the gangs that jump girls in
by running trains on them, and after that how the girls get sent out
on the stroll, whatever money they make, confiscated. Do I tell you
about the beatings? Is that too extreme? Is it, even if they happen to
nice girls like you, little middle-class sweeties whose fancy and sparkling urban lives or else whose manicured front-yard suburban lives
were supposed to shield them from the madness? Do I tell you that
none of us has built-in protection? And that protection is created,
called upon, and it arises out of truth and vigilance? If I tell you, tell
you as part of a protection spell, will I be blamed, will someone yell
at me, Why are you taking that girl's childhood away?*

So maybe no. Maybe I should take another route altogether.

*Maybe I should begin with a Barbie fascination that has morphed
grotesquely into extreme body modification and girls who have plas-*

tic surgery before they're sixteen and after that there's no stopping. Maybe I should begin with the burnings at the stake.

Or perhaps the American Constitution and Black people and women as the property of white men? Or else slavery and a population created out of rape and incest. Maybe I should begin with Thomas Jefferson.

Should I go back further? Do I begin with the Word and how the Word said it was a woman, all the fault of a woman, every sin, all that's bad, it was all our fault? I could begin there or I could begin with the Qur'an which, in the third sura, the one called Nisaa, which means, "the women," advises its reader that a man can beat his wife?

If that's too big, too much to grab hold of, I could always begin with the incredible women in your family, the women who raised me, the woman I became, the women your auntie and grandmother, became, despite it all. And I could tell you about the great-grandmother who didn't.

I mean, what is the alternative? Should I say nothing? Fly through the world on a wing, a prayer, and a couple of well-worn rules: don't give out your number; don't sit on his lap even though he's related to us; don't smile too wide, hug too close, wear your pants too tight.

How do I keep you safe, Nisa, keep you from the monsters when the truth is that the monsters are intertwined in our lives?

That's the question that visits me, night after night. It's been there from before you were born, that one question. And it should not have been. Here's what should have been the only questions to dance in my head. Here is all I ever should have wanted to know:

When will you take your first steps and where?

What will your first word be?

Will you want brothers and sisters one day?

Will you like school?

Will you be a singer, will you paint?

Will you write stories like me, or will you study theology like your father?

Will you like math or physics? Will you excel in subjects I never did grasp?

Will you be outgoing, will you be shy?

Will you be athletic?

Will you like living in Brooklyn, will you want to move to the West Coast as I did, as your auntie Anne did?

Will we survive the teenage years still loving each other? Will you learn how to drive by the time you're sixteen and will you make fun of me because I can't?

Will you learn many languages, play an instrument, visit many countries? Will you be outspoken, will you love deeply and be deeply loved in return?

Will your laughter come quickly, and will your sadness be fleeting? Will you tell me how to love you, tell me what I can do to smooth the rough borders of the landscape onto which you were born?

Will you trust me? Will you trust that whoever you are is exactly who I wanted, who I always wanted?

Will you know you are loved by me, Nisa, with everything in me that is capable of loving anyone or anything, you are loved?

And what of me? Will I be capable of ensuring the foundation upon which you can build your dreams?

Because it's not just that you are a girl who will one day be a woman in a world that has yet to prove its commitment to women. It's also that you are a Black girl. And that has its own history, its own long and painful trail.

When I began writing this letter to you, I began it in my head and I worked on it and months disappeared into years and then one day you were four. I don't know if you remember this day. We walked the Brooklyn Bridge alone together and ended up at the playground in Brooklyn Heights, one of the most expensive neighborhoods in our borough. We were the only Black people there, but I didn't notice this at first. I noticed it just at the moment a little girl took your toy away and refused to give it back to you. I held back, tried to let the two of you work it out yourselves. And when the girl ran with your toy, ran toward her mother, I encouraged you to speak: Go to her, I said. It's your right! Tell her to give it back to you, and you did that while I followed behind your scared but definite steps. You reached the girl and when you asked for the toy, she hit you, that girl. Her mother said nothing.

And in that moment, moments we have relived in various ways in various places, I had to make a decision about whether I should admonish the parent or just take you away, take you away from people who were not good enough to be around you.

Truly, I wanted to scream at that mother. I wanted to demand: What kind of child are you raising where she could hit another little girl and you do not scold her? How dare she? I wanted to say. But to argue when you are the lone Black woman or man in an unfamiliar place and you are surrounded by apparently wealthy white people, an argument is a risk because it can always spiral into something beyond your control.

In 1987, Yvonne Smallwood, a twenty-eight-year-old Black woman, was arguing about a traffic ticket when she was stomped to death by white police. We want to believe it is far outside the norm, a blip in reality, a rogue moment in the history of race and sex relations in America. But the truth is we've seen this happen again and again—whether women were arguing a traffic ticket or protesting the treatment of their children or just trying to get home. The truth is African Americans come from a long line of women who've been beaten down for speaking up.

And we, you, me come from a long line of women who were forced to live their lives with the fear that if we speak, we will lose, we will be separated from our children. From slavery to the sisters right now today, who get picked up, often on charges that are minor or else false, but because the court systems move so dreadfully slowly and because if bail is set, it is often set too high for our mothers to make, and so by the time we are released from jail, our babies have been placed in foster care. And getting our children back is much harder to accomplish than having them taken. There are records to prove this, Nisa. And there are, of course, the childless mothers. Some of them are our neighbors today, right here in Crown Heights, Brooklyn, where we make our home. I wish I didn't know these things. I wish there was no reason for me to think of them. And most of the times, I don't.

Most of the time when we are exploring the neighborhoods of New York City, or the woods of Northern California, the mountains on the Pacific Coast of Mexico, or the waters at the tip of the Long Island Sound, most of the time and in most of those places I don't see past the wonder and excitement in your face.

But there are these other times we have shared, times when I have said nothing because to speak might have consequences greater than we can manage, that I can manage. At the prison, in the playground. Wherever. And I know this must somehow all be confusing for you: me, a mommy who sometimes speaks, who is sometimes silent. Me, a mommy who has standards but then seems to abdicate them and call it strategic. And I know I cannot clear it all up for you right now. I cannot even clear it all up for myself.

Because when I became a mother, all the love I thought I always had for children, for all children, but especially a child of mine, expanded exponentially and I thought I knew what all babies deserved. I thought I knew what all babies needed. I thought I knew what you deserved and what you needed. I thought I at least would know how to protect you at every turn.

But some of what exists out there that you have not seen and some of what exists out there that you have already seen that is all tied up with you being a girl, or you being Black, or you being a Black girl in this place at this time, is not what you deserved and not what you needed and if I cannot protect you, if I cannot shield you, then do I deserve you?

deportation

When Nisa was a toddler, my girlfriend Raquel and I had a conversation about money and being a writer and not getting paid on time and what it means to be a good mother if you live in a world where it seems as though someone or something is destined to destabilize you. Some editor at a magazine was ducking her calls again for a story she'd turned in five months earlier and now the loss of that check—it was quite a substantial amount—left her spiraling into a debt she didn't know how she'd get out of. She said to me, that night on the phone, "You have to wonder what these motherfuckers would do if somebody just didn't give them their paycheck for months on end. I mean damn!"

We commiserated about not getting paid, and wondered out loud if our colleagues who made the choices not to process our payment ever considered the collateral consequences of not paying a single mother, the way it threatens, in real terms, the quality of our child's life. "And not even in the big ways," Raquel continued. "I mean I know why I don't have health care. I know why sometimes I buy food I normally wouldn't but we have to have something on the table. I mean I think about the way it affects me psychologically—"

"And then what impact that has on our daughters," I said, interrupting her, but completing her thought. But the subtext of all this is instability. Money, being paid on time and being paid a livable wage, allows a mother to plan, to think clearly. It reduces anxiety, which in turn reduces what are sometimes the results of being overanxious: smoking, overeating, drinking, compulsive shopping—the list nearly has no end.

We talk, not just my girlfriend and I, but everyone, about how children need stability, consistency. But how are they to get it if nothing in their parent's life is stable or easily stabilized? It's sort of fun and maybe even powerful to imagine that one can create anything and everything one needs in life to bring one joy and peace. But that kind of theory that keeps many people rich on the lecture circuit has little reality for people who live, in one way or another, in the margins of this society. And those people who do are usually poor, the working poor, but poor nonetheless. This is likely the relevant place to note that of all groups in society, single mothers are paid the least in every category. And no, despite the fact that fifty percent of households are now headed by single moms, no, that has not changed.

Yet, while I don't subscribe to the theory espoused generally by the privileged—that you can talk into existence whatever life you want—I do know we can work to make choices to edge ourselves up out of a hole. Money, or the lack thereof, was an anxiety that I resolved I would live with as long as I continued to choose writing as a career and pretty much be a stay-at-home mom. But what could be left behind, cast out, in the nervous breath of my world? The answer to that seemed cruel but there came a time when finally I could not avoid it.

THE *IT* IN MY own life, the one I could not avoid, happens in a phone call, like nearly everything else that has reordered my life with Rashid. I learn it via a monitored call. It is July 15, 2000. Our baby is three months and one day old.

He says he got the paperwork from INS in the mail the night before. As it stands now, he is still under a deportation order, the result of a retroactive change in law instigated by Bill Clinton in 1996. The Antiterrorism and Effective Death Penalty Act. Whenever he is finally paroled, he will likely be sent back to Guyana, the place of his birth, the only place where he holds citizenship. There can be no appeals, according to the law as it currently stands.

I said nothing to Rashid that day on the phone. What words would mean anything? Back ten years ago, when I was first falling for this beautiful Guyanese man, I asked him if there was any chance he could be deported. He assured me then that immigration issues had been taken care of. When the new law changed this in 1996, if he mentioned it to me, it was a casual thing, nothing for me to think or worry about. And I didn't. Until now. Now I feel betrayed. I want to scream, cry, use my anger toward him to make this all go away. But that's stupid, pointless. That's why I say nothing. But I'm thinking.

I'm thinking that for years that have somehow spun into a decade—and a child—I have agreed to fight alongside him, stand up for him and with him to anyone, anything. I will push back, pull forward, keep the faith even on the days when the faith wasn't keeping me. After all that work, how could this be our here and now? Rashid under a deportation order and there can be no hearing to say, But I have children in this country, a brand-new baby, a wife. No provision in the law for that, for Nisa, for me.

I am thinking these things as Rashid talks to me and I am thinking, bitterly, He sold me a lie. And that anger will sit there, it will grow tumorlike and malignant for years until it occurs to me that we all do it—that I do it—the same thing. It occurs to me one evening when I am selling Nisa the dream she most wants. It's my negotiation tactic with her: I need to write and she needs attention, she needs to make noise.

When she tells me, as she does most evenings, "Mommy, I *need* to jump and when I jump this sound *has* to come out," I know she is not lying, my wild-as-the-wind Aries girl, my tiny, magical dragon. She came into this world with so much of her personality already affixed. Early in my pregnancy when I went for a sonogram that normally takes about fifteen minutes, it became a two-day trek back and forth to the hospital for me and an ordeal for the technician, who sighed, exasperated, "She just *won't* stay still." Nisa in the womb was already who she was destined to be. That I know.

Which is another reason why I try more often than not to negotiate with her rather than yell at her to be quiet. On many a night, many a day, you can hear me and I am saying to her that Mommy is trying to figure it all out: how to buy her house, a home with more than one floor, a backyard big enough to put a swing set in. And, of course, this biggest of all promises: her very own puppy. I tell Nisa to trust me, I'm trying. I tell her if we work together as a team, we can make them happen, the dreams we have for ourselves.

That's when it occurs to me that I am doing to my baby what was done to me: the offering up of the idea of a life, a bigger life, a life outsize in its proportion of joy, if only she has faith, hope, an impossible sort of patience and perseverance, even on this one brilliant summer weekend when I am writing and she is holed up in the house. And as I settle into this practice, this practice of negotiating in what I would only consider good faith, I finally get it, finally I realize what Rashid did with me.

He asked me to hold on, to hold out for a dream he thought he could really make happen. He'd asked me before and then again, that July fifteenth: "Just hang in there, baby. I am going to fix it. I promise you. I *promise* you." I said okay. I said I would, but there was nothing inside of me that allowed me to make a rational decision in the wake of that news. In the wake of disaster, we may say anything to send it all away—the unfolding reality before us. But a few days out, shock and denial turned to anger and it would be years before it diffused. Years and years.

At first I said OK. I said I could endure it, fight it with him. I mean, what else had I ever done? But then I found I couldn't even say the word, the terrible, brutal, life-altering word, *deportation,* without my throat, my stomach tightening, without feeling as though I might lose my ability to breathe right then, right there. When he called in the days just after, I changed my tone, though slightly. All I could say to Rashid, all I could say to myself was this: I can't. Can't talk, can't think, can't plan, can't stay, can't run. I can't believe. That was the bottom line. I couldn't believe. I did not say that aloud though. Not to him. Not to myself.

When I was able to lurch toward some level of engagement

with Rashid, then all I could say was, I'm tired. But of course that described nothing. If I were simply tired, I could get in bed, rest, sleep, come back out swinging the very next day. But there was no next day, there was no nothing. Nothing for us, nothing for Rashid, nothing for our family.

There would be no more fantasizing about the day we would be there, standing at the prison gate one morning, waiting as Rashid exits the facility for the final time. No more dream of walking these Brooklyn streets together doing what normal couples do—errands, a stroll in the park, playing hooky and sneaking in a weekday matinee and a slice of pizza afterward. There would be no coming-home party, no looking for a house together, no fashioning an oasis inside a concrete box in an over-priced apartment in an overpriced city. No lounging in bed together—our own bed, not a prison bed—with my family on some rainy or cold Saturday morning, reading the paper, making hot chocolate, eating popcorn, watching videos. No more hope that there will be more babies, maybe a dog.

It was all gone. All the dreams, all the stories that I had told myself for ten years, the stories I told to sustain myself, every part of them, eviscerated. And they were gone at the very moment that they most needed to be here, because here was Nisa and when we knew she was coming, we talked it through and we agreed yes, the first couple of years of her life, Rashid would be away, the first couple of years would be challenging, but what beauty lay on the other side of patience! Nisa's memory of her father would not be shaped by distance and bars.

And that's how we did it, that's how I did it, that's how I made it through the nine months alone but not lonely, alone but not broken. It's how I made it through labor and birth. That's how I did not lose my composure when I came back to my apartment with my baby that first night, the night without my husband, and all we had was the phone and he called and sang the "Adon" in her ear and we felt close and we felt as though, no, no, everything wasn't as we wanted it, but that part, the as-we-wanted part, it was just around the corner. This is how I kept my sanity in proximity.

But now, what? What do we say to ourselves in order to make it across the rocky days? What tool did I have? These are the questions I would not ask of Rashid, the words I would not speak. That every piece of the life we had knitted together over the last ten years, everything we waited for, everything we believed in, sacrificed for, were gone. And if all our dreams were gone, all the dreams and all the pieces of dreams, then how could I not be gone too?

I asked girlfriends, a therapist, anyone who would listen, that very question. "Because of Nisa," was always the quick answer shot back at me. And of course, of course. I wanted my love for Nisa to be enough to set aside the hurt, to crowd it out. And of course I did everything I could to compensate for all I was feeling. And of course too, it wasn't enough. Not really.

∼

I MET A YOUNG man once who had only recently reintroduced himself to his son. He kept the child now every weekend, and from what I could see, he appeared to be a very devoted and loving father. But as we chatted, he went on to confess to me that he had hit a rough patch, and during that time—a year, he told me—he didn't see his boy. According to him, he hadn't been involved in his son's life at all, not emotionally, physically, or financially. For mothers, for most of us anyway, there's no such option, no way to check out for a year or so while we get ourselves together, grieve, organize our finances, meditate, teach ourselves to breathe again. I don't imagine that many of us would even want that, but if we did, where would we go to take a break?

As much as I wanted to crawl under a bed, hide in a closet, escape, I couldn't. Both the joy and demands of motherhood each day grew bigger and more complex, and they required my presence. And I was, present. I was present at least during the day, during the hours in which responsibilities spiraled way over my head. I wrote and edited articles, books, maintained a modicum of my political activism, took Nisa to gardens, to museums, to libraries and playgrounds. I worked out, learned how to make (though I rarely did) organic baby food. I visited my parents most Sundays, traveled several times with Nisa in her first years of life to report stories or give lectures.

I was in the world. I was in it until the sun went down and the baby went to sleep and stories were filed and the phone calls were returned, and then, not immediately, but after a time when the pain swelled so large it felt as though I could not move or think, conscious or not, I fell into a half-life, a life checked out, a deported life, a life sent away by sweet wine, glasses and glasses of it, sweet wine and cigarettes. They transported me, but where? They allowed me to pass out, to not think about what had gone away. They allowed me to sleep without dreaming until the alarm went off and it was time to rise and pretend to be more than I was, more than I was perhaps even capable of being. It was time to pretend that nothing, not the separation, not the deportation, nothing, cut or crippled me.

But before this, before I can recognize the way my sadness is forming a fence around my heart, before we're headlong into some new, distanced reality, Rashid calls me. It's September of 2000. Nisa is five months old.

"I know things are hard, baby," he begins, "but they're going to get better. I'm going to beat this thing and be home with you and Nisa." I hate to hear him say this because I am trying to come to terms with the new configuration of my life. I am trying to consider how to have new dreams. And yet I cannot stop listening.

"We've been issued a date for a trailer," he continues. "Please. Just come up. Let's spend some real family time together. Let me take care of you and my daughter. Let me spoil you for two days, baby," he says, and I'm right there again, right in the center of hope, right back in a life I thought I'd have to leave behind. But maybe. Maybe things will work out. Maybe we can love it all away.

Maybe he has a real plan he can only tell me in whispers, alone in a trailer on a prison compound. Maybe we are meant to be together, a couple, a family. Maybe we can overcome the deportation order. Maybe the law will change. Maybe parole will work out. Maybe everything we promised each other and believed during our long courtship and five-year marriage will come to pass. I tell him what I always wound up telling him: Yes, baby. I'll be there. I pack up food, clothes, diapers, sheets, toiletries, the baby, and me. I hire a car and head up to the prison.

How do you know, do you ever really know, that the last time with someone is really the last time? Is it ever possible to conceive such a thing when it is late and quiet and the entire of the world has briefly contracted, and now, now the world is no bigger, no more complicated than a size that you and your tiny little family can manage, and he is touching you? He has spent the day touching some part of you and Nisa, almost in disbelief that you are alive and real, not some hologram, some mirage. We could not have conceived then, neither Rashid nor I, that our first conjugal visit as a family would also be our last. I'm sure of that.

During that visit, that easy, that calm, that beautiful, that life-giving visit, Rashid watches everything Nisa and I do with the eyes of someone who has gone blind and through some sudden miracle—not a medical one so much as an otherworldly one but a miracle nonetheless—he has been regranted the gift of sight. The way I breast-feed, the way Nisa nestles in my arms, flapping her arms, studying her surroundings, relaxing when she's rocked, this is all new to him, and if I am to understand the wonder I see in his eyes, we are nearly holy. He bathes us and he washes our hair and he cooks for me and feeds me, a fork he lifts to my mouth. He changes Nisa and insists he be the one to hold her until she falls asleep, which she finally does on his chest, moving peacefully with the rhythm of his breathing.

He places her in a crib in the next room and comes back to me and this is when we make love, late, late into the visit, so unlike our other visits, our pre-Nisa life when sex was immediate and constant and wild. Now it happens on our daughter's clock, and we laugh about this and we embrace the change. But finally when we are certain Nisa will sleep for at least a couple of hours, this is when it happens.

Somehow, then, that time, it was more intimate, our sex, more musical. It was nearly like a rescue, the way we made love, the kind of touching where you leave nothing behind. You leave everything right there in your lover's hands, his mouth. We were more generous than we'd ever been, more gracious, and when we moved together we cried, both of us did, to know how this is what we needed, how this was what we needed daily, how this was what kept us in contact with our own humanity, in contact with the best of ourselves. And yet it was exactly this thing that we could not have.

But for forty-four hours in September of 2000, we did, we had it. Deportation was set aside; parole issues and money issues, they were beyond our consciousness. We set aside everything, everything that was hard, we didn't even glance at them and we really lived, however briefly, however falsely even, but for us, we lived a lifetime in a moment, and a moment in the space we had always sought to occupy. For forty-four hours, the world was animate and it was ours and everywhere it was safe and everywhere it was shining.

In short, we sipped the wine. Perhaps we should not have. Because as the old adage warned, the sipping made it all the worse. It made it all the more shocking when we could not have it the night after that or the night after that. It was more shocking than even before, before we had a child, because now Rashid's presence was bigger than my desire for him. Now there were two of us and desire was coupled with absolute need and that need could not be fulfilled and although logically I

77

understand that I should not have been shocked, I was. I could not believe that I would not wake the next morning and find him there, there with us, and suddenly one night became two and two nights became years.

Years passed and that September became a memory that recessed into the shadows and I realized that yes, wow, that time back then was the last time for us and had we known, had I known, I would have surely have marked the date on the calendar, noted it as a sad anniversary each year, observed a moment of silence, told close friends and loved ones about what happened. I surely would have mourned.

But none of that happened and we spent those forty-four hours and perhaps even a short time after as though we, us, our family was going to be possible. Rashid spoke in defiant terms about beating the deportation order and was just as certain he would make parole. And after our visit, briefly I was a believer again. Encouraged by my perennially optimistic husband, I started thinking about how I could juggle work, parenting, writing, and a husband who was in prison. He wouldn't be there for very much longer, I told myself.

But it was then, in the midst of those thoughts, that the reality of our life came along and made things all so simple. Rashid was transferred to a prison nearly impossible to get to. Never in all the years that we had been together, in all of the years before he became Nisa's father, had Rashid ever been made so inaccessible.

As always, I receive the news like this: I get a phone call from one of Rashid's friends, who says, "He's in the box." He offers no real explanations, makes nothing clear.

As of that call, I had known Rashid for more than ten years, been his wife for more than five. We'd run up thousands and thousands of dollars in phone bills, spent countless hours in conversation with one another, speaking, sharing. But in all that time, across all those years, never had I heard those words, the ones that I'd always feared, the ones that meant that Rashid would be locked in special unit, alone, for twenty-three hours a day. The other hour was allowed for exercise in an outdoor cage. Alone.

Phone calls were banned. Our only communication was letter writing, which was much harder for me now with a job and a daughter. The fissure that grew between us was nearly one you could see. Without visits or real-time communication, Rashid's life in a prison no longer was something I could understand or make sense of. And my life doing a slow redaction into working, parenting, cleaning, bill paying, sleeping, working, cleaning some more, was not one he could understand.

Our worlds, and so the two of us, became unknown, unknowable to one another. And Nisa and Rashid became distanced as well. Important milestones—her first steps—could not even be shared over the phone. Fatherhood via fiber optics and weekend visits was not even possible. Months would pass before we were able to get there, up to the new facility, so that Nisa could visit her father, my husband, this stranger.

Eventually letters from Rashid came that told a bizarre story about how he was accused of being the mastermind behind a stabbing incident in the prison. Rashid and five others were convened before a prison panel and found guilty of stabbing another member of their Muslim community. Never mind that the only evidence against Rashid and the others was secret and—to this day—uncorroborated testimony. Never mind that the minor wound on the victim hardly corresponded with his story of being attacked by several men. Never mind that it was public knowledge that the so-called victim disliked Rashid intensely because Rashid was considered a leader in the community. And never mind that in the end, the court system, months after Rashid finished his time in the box, every day of it, found him innocent of all charges.

But that's getting ahead.

In the days following the false incident, prison officials sentenced Rashid to 120 days in isolation and before you could say, *Whoa, Nellie, where's the goddamn evidence?* he was shipped an unimaginable nine hours away to a new facility in a part of the state neither of us had ever heard of before. This is what happened in the time following the time we were on the trailer in September. This is what happened that took our hope apart. That took us apart.

"It's a total lockdown joint," Rashid writes me, in a letter from his new address. "Everybody here is in the box. That's how they're building prisons now," he writes. "We're locked in cells that are the same size as single cells everywhere else, but here it's all double-bunked. Can you imagine being locked up in a room the size of your bathroom, with a stranger? For months? For something you didn't do?"

I am at work as I read this. I am trying to live this new life as a mother, as a magazine editor. And I am trying to do it with a measure of competency and cool, but here is my reality. I am sitting in a cubicle waiting for Denzel Washington to call back on a story I am writing, but no matter how hard I am pushing for this new life, looking dignified and hip at the same time sitting in a cubicle, I am snatched back into the old one. And as much as I love Rashid, I don't want to be. I don't want to spend my days and nights worried about the world of prisons and guards but I can't imagine leaving this man alone, this man I made a child with. I want to curl up in a corner, sob, scream. I want to call a friend, tell her what's happening. But I am at work. I am a mother. I cannot lose it. At work there is professional decorum. At home there is my baby, and my loss of calm destroys hers. Of course out in the street if you lose it and you're Black, you're doing time. I tell no one what's happening, not for some time, not until I trust I can say the words, but devoid of emotion.

The transformation into that person, the one without feelings, begins on the subway ride home as I finish reading the rest of the letter. On that 3 train speeding toward Brooklyn, it may look like me, but it isn't me. It is someone else, an impostor, a pod person. She can walk through the world without reaction, and certainly without tears. I let her take in the information, consider it, but not process it. I let her go home, breast-feed my child, go to sleep in my bed. Me, the real asha, has already ferreted out a hiding place and stored myself there, while a Stepford mother, worker, woman, wife, moves about in my stead. She deals with everything, including the words contained in Rashid's letter:

"If you want to come see me, just so you know, visits here are at night from 6 to 9 PM." After that he adds, "You cannot come see me the first 30 days though. The first 30 days here, all visits are behind the glass. And I'd have to be shackled. Leg irons and cuffs. You and my daughter can't see me like that. But after 30 days—now only 22!—I can be at a table with you. That's if you want to come."

I knew I would make the trip and Rashid did too. Despite my decision to retreat from half of my life being spent behind prison walls, my need to keep prisons from institutionalizing my child, I could not let Rashid sit in a cell for four months with no outside contact, no outside confirmation that he was still alive and that he mattered and that he would always matter. To me, certainly, but most of all to our daughter.

Chapter 6

---

crash

We leave the house, Nisa and D and I, like fugitives under the dark weight of night, quietly slipping out of my apartment building sometime before four in the morning. Rashid's father and best friend had offered to split the nine-hour drive upstate so that Nisa could see her dad. So that he could see her. The night before we were to leave, Rashid's dad backed out, but D did not, and together we began the nine-hour journey to a place none of us would ever, in a world we made, a world we had control over, choose as a destination. It was March 3, 2001, and the weatherman was predicting a horrible snowstorm that weekend, but I didn't learn this until after.

Later, when my parents asked me what happened, how did things go wrong on that trip to see Rashid, I said to them that all I remembered was telling D I was getting tired, that I didn't think I could stay awake with him any longer. I suggested to him that we pull over; we had already been driving about seven and a half hours and we had plenty of time to rest by the side of the road for a little while and still arrive at our hotel, put our things away, freshen up, eat, and head over to the facility on time. He said, no, no. Just like that. "No, no. I got this. Go to sleep, baby girl." After that, I said to my mother, all I remember is screaming, begging him to get control of the vehicle; he was not able to do it.

We hydroplaned, flipped, went over a thirty-foot ravine, cut down four or five trees, and the car broke into three parts before finally stopping. And then suddenly there was a man standing over us, a stranger who had seen the accident. "I don't think there are any survivors here," he said. "No," I mumbled at him, I think, anyway, that the word came out. I struggled to get myself loose, screamed for them to help my baby, who was strapped tight in her car seat in the back.

The stranger helped me out of the car and I ran, stumbled, ran some more, stumbled some more, over to the other side of the car to get to my baby, to pull her out of the wreckage and then back up the hill where paramedics were already arriving. D followed behind us a few minutes later. I kept thinking that the car was going to blow up just like in the movies. It's real, you know, the thing that takes over you, the superhuman strength thing, when you think your child's life is on the line. I'm sure I've never moved so fast in my life, certain as I was that there was going to be an explosion.

When we reach the top of the ravine, the paramedics strap me onto a board and they separate Nisa from me. I don't know where she is. The paramedic brings her over but I cannot touch her. I am strapped down. There is a fear that something is broken and they want to keep me immobilized. I don't remember how D was taken out of the car, or how he gets to the hospital, and I don't remember if Nisa and I ride in the same ambulance. I don't remember seeing my baby again until we are in the hospital. They bring her to me finally and place her on my chest and it's only then that her screams stop. We are, all of us, x-rayed and examined and determined to be fine, considering.

D has a bruised rib cage, I have a concussion, but Nisa is completely without physical injury. It is four-thirty in the afternoon. A police officer is there and I ask him to call the prison, to tell my husband what's happened. I give him the phone number, Rashid's information. "Please tell him that we're fine," I nearly plead, "but we will not be able to see him." All I can think of is that I want to be home. I want to be safe, alone and safe with my daughter. When the cop saunters back toward us about fifteen minutes later, I ask if he's called the facility. "Yup," he responds. I ask if he said that we were fine despite the accident. Calmly, he looks at me and says, "I just told him that there was an accident and y'all wouldn't be coming."

Of course we have to go now. Now there is no choice, no way we can rest. If Rashid does not see us, if he does not hear anything more—and there will be no way for him to know more before we are back home—he will cave in to worry. Something bad happening to a family member is a major fear for men in prison I have known. Rashid and I will never forget the day a man's wife, in a freak accident, fell out of a moving van on the highway on the way to see her husband. She did not survive. I could not let Rashid have any of those fears, especially about his baby, a baby under a year old. Where does additional anxiety take a man, I wonder, who is already in hell?

From the hospital I call a taxi service and a guy who could have been a body double for one of the mountain men from the film *Deliverance* shows up in a car I thought he would have to turn a crank on to get running. But he seems nice enough and besides, we are desperate. "You know how to get to the prison?" I asked him. "Sure do," he responds, not cheerfully, but neither does he sound judgmental. He gets us to the facility safe and sound, and exactly on time, just as a van of other wives, mothers, sisters, and daughters are unloading packages and getting themselves signed in and processed through metal detectors.

I have almost no memory of that place, what it looked like, how we were treated by the guards, if we ate from the vending machine, if Rashid was waiting for us when we walked in, if we had to wait for a long time for him to come to the visiting room. That whole visit, nearly the whole of it, happened someplace outside of me, someplace that does not normally store memory. There are just small snatches of images: Rashid holding me, holding us, Nisa and me. He told me that when the facility informed him of the accident, he thought things had been much worse, that he hadn't been given much information.

After I tell him the details of the accident, Rashid shakes his head, holds us tighter, tells me he cannot believe we are there, with him. D is sitting at the table with us. I'm sure they talked. I don't know what about. And then Rashid says, I suppose for emphasis, "I just can't believe after everything that's happened, you're here. You're here and you're looking at me like you used to look at me."

"What do you mean?" I ask.

"I mean you're looking at me like you need me."

I don't respond. Maybe I do need him. Maybe I do not. I have no idea at that moment, nor did I the day before that or the day before that, what I need.

When the visit comes to an end, Deliverance is waiting, as promised, right outside the prison door. The snow, already swirling above and around us, seems now poised to rage. The airports have been closed, as has the bus station. There is no train service in this part of New York State. Deliverance is our only hope for getting home in the next twenty-four hours. I can't believe I'm willing to get in a car for hours and hours again, that I'm willing to ride those roads, but I need my home, my own warm place with its multicolored walls, its mud-cloth prints, the pillows and the candles and the peace lily and the ivy; and my home with the all its books, the Dexter Gordon CDs, the yellow-and-purple sheets Nisa and I curl up in, the notebooks I write in. I needed to be near it all. I needed to feel safe, and I could not feel safe in this place, this place of prisons and crashes.

We negotiate with Deliverance's taxi company. Nine hundred dollars and the deal is done. We have a ride home, which we are ready for first thing the next morning. Deliverance shows up with a friend, also someone who would qualify for mountain man body-double status. This doesn't feel like the smartest decision I have ever made, but what choice do we have?

D and I look at the two young tattooed men, and we all shake hands and get in the car, which, you can't make this up, they called their company's luxury vehicle—a gray and rust-stained Caddy, circa 1972. I look at the vehicle. Unlike the other, I don't think it needs a crank, but I wonder how much gas the boat-sized thing takes. D, Nisa, and I ride in the back. I place Nisa gently in her car seat, which had been one of the few things—besides us—left relatively intact after the crash.

Still, I say a prayer, whisper it into Nisa's ear. The boys turn on the radio. Black Sabbath is playing. I don't know what I was hoping for—maybe a little Donnie McClurkin? I buckle up. Double-check Nisa's straps.

We're about fifteen minutes into the trip back to New York City when Deliverance's dispatcher two-way-radios him and says the price of the ride is double and if we can't pay, no trip. Deliverance, and his friend—who also works for the service—argue vehemently with their boss. "A deal is a deal," one of them says. Their boss tells them if we don't pay now—and if they don't drop that money off at the base before heading south to the city—they would both be fired.

More words are exchanged, and then suddenly—it was Deliverance who said it, tossing his long, blond hair around defiantly—"Fuck it, man. We're going to New York." With that, he turns off the two-way, turns up Black Sabbath, and together the two of them navigate us safely back to our home.

What those two days will teach me, beyond reminding me not to judge people right off the bat—and that was a big one—what I will carry for the next three years, is some sort of scattered lesson, one with no real beginning, no real end, only a whirling dervish of fear, hazy but repeating, and brutal images of the entire end of the world I know, the streets and the people and parks and waters and the loves and my baby, my baby, snatched up by giant enemy arms, snatched up and thrown, crashed to the ground, and all of them, all of us splitting apart, breaking, broken. No survivors. The lesson that sat in me, in my bones, in my blood, waiting there like a slow-moving poison, was one of danger lurking everywhere, but nowhere more so than with Rashid.

The lesson I should have taken, but the one that will not occur to me until I sit down to write this story, is that I can make my way home, I have always made my way home, no matter what the challenge, no matter how icy the road. And I can do it not only because I am invested in doing it, invested even when I am not conscious of it, but also because there are others, there are people, human beings, who, despite a million real or meaningless differences that may exist between us, those people, those humans, agree—and sometimes it is for just one brief moment, and sometimes it is as a life's commitment—that yes, we do, each one of us, deserve the chance to get back home.

not love, actually

I can still hear my mother's voice admonishing eight-year-old me to slow down, to pay attention. Me, a girl, forever trying to run a circle around the wind. I rushed through school, I rushed through my schoolwork and childhood and childhood's friends, and now at thirty-three, I was rushing through the end of a marriage. It made me wonder, though I will never know, was I born early too, did I rush even then, before I knew word or concept? But whether it was a genetic or learned trait, I knew I wanted to move on, to heal the hurt, build a new life for me, for Nisa.

I'm trying to say I fell in love again, quickly and thoroughly, not long after Rashid and I broke up.

I close my eyes even now and see him, Amir, his walk that made him seem bigger than he was, his brilliant smile, his even more brilliant mind. The first time we met, he said to me, "Forgive me for staring at you. You're just so beautiful." And it wasn't the words so much as the way he let it go right afterward. He didn't do what most men I've known have done: decide that they like the way you look, that they want a relationship, and that they will pursue it regardless of your feelings. It was

different with this man. I felt then, right there in the beginning, respected. Those words, his words, they made me believe that after a childhood in which so many boundaries had
been violated, and after time with a man in prison where the
boundaries of our life were violated, finally I was safe. I was
safe with this man who early on held my face and said nothing
bad would happen to me again, that he would see to it, that he
would, "bleed for me," if need be. How could I not want him?
And then one day he said to me, "And you know I love Nisa."

In the time after the deportation order, Amir and I talked
about the future of the world and the future of our world and
our hopes mirrored each other's. "Do you want more children,"
he asked me once, and I said yes. And he asked me if I would
ever consider being a stay-at-home mom and I said yes. And he
asked me if I would ever consider moving away from the city
and I said yes. And then he said he still wanted to go slowly—
before making the full-on commitment—and that surprised
me. But I said yes.

In those first months following the end of my marriage, I
spent weekends with Nisa and Amir walking across the New
York autumn. South Street Seaport, Prospect Park, long drives
upstate, we would lose ourselves in the colors that it seemed I
was experiencing for the first time in years because for the first
time in years, I was experiencing them while holding the hand
of a man I loved.

I had never had such a time with Rashid. Never had these
simple moments. Not even during my first marriage, really.
I'd never had the simple romance of sharing a day, letting the
hours fall where they would, answering to no one but ourselves.

And when I had nighttime child care, as I did once a week back then, Amir and I did something else that was brand new to me and sexy. We went to lounges, to clubs together, a couple. We danced fast or slow, but we always connected, legs and arms cobbled together on dark floors. We drank great wines and toasted each other and toasted love. We named the son we imagined we would one day have together, the baby brother Nisa would help guide. We kissed in darkened doorways and then later in the back of taxis because waiting until we were home was too long a wait.

We made love in public places, in bathrooms in fancy restaurants. We talked every day. We made career decisions together—he was a Wall Streeter. We talked about books I would write, screenplays, how he could help with financing. When career challenges presented, we supported each other. And yes, yes I thought about Rashid and what we'd had and what we'd lost, and there were many times when I felt the strangle of guilt. But greater than that discomfort, greater than the pain of the end of a marriage, was the sense that I needed someone who could understand the contours of my life. Amir seemed like that person, the one who understood the contours of my life. And I was certain I understood the contours of his. We even declared as much, our emotions nearly choking another. We said our minds were twin engines. We discussed creating our own human rights organization. We talked about the world as we wanted to see it. "I'm sick of our people suffering," he said, frustration in his voice when we talked about the Amadou Diallo case that was being played out in the media at the time. "Just so damn sick of it," he said, even more emotion brimming, and I knew he was thinking about the boys on the block he came up with, so many of whom were dead, others in prison, others still wandering the neighborhood, shouting to passersby. I think it's likely true that he'd seen more death and destruction before he was ten than I have even now, as of this day—which is saying something given that not long after Nisa was born, in one year alone, fourteen people I knew, many of whom I loved, died. Only one, my aunt Mary, was elderly. But everyone else hovered at just about fifty, except the man who would have been Nisa's godfather, Taheem. He didn't make it to thirty-five.

I knew death and I knew loss and so I knew when someone had the same weight in their heart that I had in mine. He had it. And I wanted to heal it. I wanted to heal it for him and I wanted to heal it for me. We began sharing the details of our lives. He told me of his missing father, the one he looked so much like. I told him of my missing childhood.

I told him about what happened with the molestations and I didn't worry when he didn't seem too turned around by it. I didn't want to compare him to Rashid, who had so much pathos for me, offered so much support. Amir was different and that was okay. It was okay, I told myself this, that he seemed to relegate my past to the past, because, after all, wasn't that where it belonged? Even if his past was right there in the anger that crouched right behind his beautiful brown eyes, that had nothing to do with me. I was moving on. And my job was to help him do the same so we could walk together into a perfect tomorrow.

And you know, it wasn't as though I never noticed the anger that pulsed in him. It was that, first, the anger wasn't all there was to see, and second, I never took that anger as something that would be directed toward me, his partner. The snide remarks he would make, the mean little jokes he would slip in about everything from the way I talked or laughed to the way I cooked, who takes these things seriously? Who takes them seriously when the whole package includes something you never had before: a lover who was present and daily and who you were politically and emotionally and physically in tune with?

Amir was the first man I ever experienced full-blown, adult romance with. My first marriage was not a romantic affair to be sure, and besides, I was a teenager, literally, when I became engaged, barely a woman, twenty-one, when I married. And of course with Rashid, well, with Rashid there was the prison. But here I was, thirty-three years old with a new baby and, like it or not, a new life. And now I was in places with this pretty man whom I could be with whenever we wanted, whenever *I* wanted. I could make love to him whenever, wherever. So surely I need not focus on a few misplaced and poor jabs. This is what I told myself, what I told friends, one in particular who just kept repeating, "There's just something about him that makes me uncomfortable." She, like most others, never heard his sarcasm. They would just meet him and feel chilled, tell me he simply seemed "off."

"He's shy," I would say, defending my man, "and hard to get to know," I continued, dismissing her concern, preferring instead the approval of strangers, waiters and others who would meet us in our fancy places and love "a young, beautiful Black couple who was making it happen." Amir and I were told that, again and again. And in the dark, sexy places, the places blurred by wine and both real and imagined romance, I believed.

I believed it especially as my work as an author and journalist seemed to take its own shape and I continually found myself in elite places, places of celebrity and star shine. Viewed through the lens of my own life, it seemed everything was spiraling up. After the hard mean drop, with my baby on my back, I was headed back up a mountain. But that was the lens that I looked through. For Amir the lens opened onto quite another landscape. His own career was struggling. Much of it wasn't his fault. The nuances of the economy—and he being most junior in the firms he joined—saw him laid off more than once. That was hard. The effort to find other jobs though—that seemed impossible. Months and months went by without work or callbacks. Or money. And I should have realized. As much as women are often defined by others and our own selves by what we look like, men are judged by status and money. But the removal of both is, for many, the removal of their whole humanity. I didn't see things quite that way then. I just wanted, as any woman in love would want, to help. I had connections, knew people who knew people. Reluctantly at first, and then finally, he accepted. He accepted after I convinced him that by helping him I wasn't also challenging his manhood.

"Of course you don't need me to make things right for you," I argued one afternoon. "But if I can help, why shouldn't I?"

"You act like I can't do this on my own," he responded, his voice thick with anger.

"That's not true," I said, in what became a back and forth until at last agreement. We had been dating for under a year. And his reaction was my first glimpse of the full space of the anger that resided in his heart. Because it wasn't only that he expressed resentment at my offer of help. He also took that chance to go on a tangent that would characterize the rest of our relationship. Why were things okay for me but rough for him? Inevitably, unbelievably, in language I could not retain it was so mean, he began to insinuate that I was where I was because I was fucking my way into assignments, because I was a slut.

Worse than the indignity of the name-calling was that it was he, not I, who was not monogamous! He saw that as the whole part of the "not making a commitment" thing, justified by the fact that I'd only recently separated from Rashid. Whatever hearing I gave that the first month or second, as time stacked up and the romance stacked up it seemed less and less a legitimate excuse. But he insisted and I wasn't ready to lose someone again. So yes, he kept sleeping with a bunch of other women all the while calling me a slut.

And I accepted it. I accepted it because I thought if I loved openly and with the whole of my heart I could change him. Our good times were, after all, so very good. It had to work out! When Amir accused me of lying about my commitment to him, instead of walking—or running—away, I just defended myself, did everything to prove it wasn't true. Everything to prove I was a good girl. A girl—not like the baby I once was—a baby worth keeping.

⁓

IN THE EARLY SUMMER of 2001, I was able to maneuver a meeting between Amir and one of the most famous and respected men in finance. It was a coup. In a downtown office, the two men talked for an hour and a half while I wandered in and out of cheap stores in lower Manhattan, the ones that sell dresses for ten dollars a pop. When finally my cell phone rang and it was Amir saying he was leaving the building and I needed to come back around the corner and meet him, I nearly floated there. An hour and a half? Who has meetings that long? I was certain something would happen and that a new picture-framed life, a life that had been shunted by the prisons, was coming into focus. We glided through the rest of the day, picked up Nisa, went out to dinner, toasted our future, made love through the night, made love the next morning. For much of the rest of the summer, we lived like this: squinting down the road to see where hope was waiting.

If you were to hear him tell it, it was me who screwed it all up that August. Here's what went down: I asked him if he'd ever written a thank-you note to my mentor, the one who'd set up the meeting.

"Why would I do that," Amir growled, six weeks—perhaps a lifetime—of fury shooting forward at me. "I didn't get a damn job!"

"I know," I countered, trying to calm him down, "but she couldn't guarantee you a job. She did everything she said she would. She made the calls and set up the meeting. And you got the meeting. The thank-you note is for that."

"You're such an ass-kisser. No wonder everyone loves you."

He said this.

And that was it. We were off and fighting. We'd been in his car driving out of the city for the day, a late summer retreat. But before we'd made it out of Brooklyn, he was turning the car around and he was speeding back toward my apartment, and then I was home, stomping up the stairs and through my front door. For the rest of the afternoon, in between crying jags, I called him, alternately cursing him and then asking, Why would you treat someone who loves you like this? He told me to stop. Said if I didn't, he would make me.

"Make me then, motherfucker," I said, all Brooklyn-girl defiance in my voice.

And he did. He came over that night. Nisa was asleep. When my doorbell rang and I knew it was Amir, I assumed we would argue but then we would make up. I assumed we would fall into bed together, proclaim our love once more, make it all better. I mean, isn't that how it goes? Isn't that what it is between people who love each other? And wasn't that our pattern? So no, no I didn't think about the names he'd called me for months, for years, accusing me of the very behaviors he was engaging in.

And yes, we'd even had some troubling physical encounters. The worst of them though had confused me about, more than clarified, the rage he held. We would play-fight, wrestle—but the way lovers do—as foreplay. During those "games," he dragged me down my hallway by my hair—versions of this happened twice, maybe three or four times. Years on, they all become one long nasty incident. But he used to drag me down the hallway and slam my head into the wall and laugh, but I didn't. I said for him to stop. I said he was playing too roughly. It took a long time, after everything was said and done, to see those interactions as something far uglier than playing too roughly. But back then, labeling them as I did, as play, meant I had no reason to tell him to go. No reason to go through yet one more loss. He said he loved my daughter. He said he loved me. And I clung to that even when my hairstylist or manicurist would stare at the chunks of hair I was suddenly missing, the broken nails, and at least once, scratches down my face. I don't remember anymore how I responded when they looked at me one day and gasped, "What happened?!" I remember only that I said to myself again and again, We were just playing.

Anyway, that's how we got to that hot August night, and how I could let him in without being prepared for all that would happen, even after he had threatened me.

I wasn't prepared when he grabbed me and rushed me down to the floor of my living room, my foot catching and twisting under the base of my sofa on the way. It snapped apart, my foot did, but I didn't know. I was in shock. It hurt but I thought it was a sprain. I didn't find out until the next day when two friends took me to the hospital. It was a compound fracture; my entire foot was shattered. A month later when the swelling went down enough for surgeons to rebuild my foot, the chief of podiatric surgery asked me if they could take pictures for a book he was working on. He said he had never seen damage so complete. And then I went under and woke up eight hours later in a cast I wore for the next two months.

And Amir did apologize, finally, although he was just as quick to remind me it was my calls that made him do it, and that he never meant to hurt me like that. I wanted to believe him, but eventually his words felt like the harsh grip of his hands, the ones that put me on the floor that night, the ones that held me there, his hands tight over my mouth, telling me I was going to learn to watch what I say.

People always think domestic violence is a no-brainer. One

slap and you're out. That's not how it works in real life, I don't care what your politics are. When you fall in love with someone or when you believe you're in love with someone, you don't just get out because getting out makes sense. What seems to make more sense is that if *you* get your act together, *you* can make everything beautiful again. Because once things were beautiful. You are an addict reaching back to reclaim that first great high, love, with all its opening up of pleasure receptors in the brain, just as dysfunctional as a person who's struggling with drugs or alcohol. So yes, we tried to work things out after the terrible August night. But finally I learned that there are places you cannot make it back from, not with everything you started with anyway.

Still there are times, there were times when I'd ask, Where was my king, my beautiful Black man who talked about babies with me? In the very start of our relationship, before he'd invested himself in making cutting remarks toward me, before the job trouble started. Where was that man, the one who said he would protect me, bleed for me?

Because despite the way he came to see my career as a thriving thing, a thing in opposition to him, the truth is that I had a terrible boss, a mean woman who seemed to make it her business to hurt people. I wasn't singled out. I was just one of many, and when I would come home hurt or angry, it was his arms that held me. When I worried about bills, about any of the normal downward shifts that impose upon a life, it was him, swashbuckling across my insecurities. When we started, not a day passed when Amir wouldn't whisper, "You are an incredible woman, asha." No man in my life had made me feel valid in *quite* that way. Not in real life where I could come home to it every day. Amir was Superman to me. In the beginning.

In the weeks and months after the deportation order and after the end of the marriage that had meant the world to me, but to no one else, he, this new man, stepped in and said I counted and made me feel as though there was a coming tomorrow that would erase the sad yesterday. He said things that bolstered and renewed me at the very time, the very hour when I was sure I didn't matter much anymore, couldn't be renewed.

Before we became a couple, I was sure, in the face of the prison, in the face of the law, that I didn't matter. That I didn't count and neither did my baby. After all, this is what the law says, in fact, not simply by implication: that Nisa and I did not count. In a sense, that's what had been the enduring message in my head: You do not count. From a mother who took a pass on me to a prison system that would eventually do likewise to both me and my baby. We didn't count. To a trained counselor or even a home-girl from around the way, these may all sound like excuses, but I know where my heart was when we began. Amir said both Nisa and I counted, and these words were oxygen to me.

So yes, I stayed after I should have left. I stayed almost a year trying to get it all back. But then one night I had a conversation with my mother, my real mother, the woman who raised me. And she talked to me about a night she remembered the first week my foot was broken. She said, remember before Nisa's babysitter left for the evening, and she put the baby to sleep in her crib in her room, and when you were completely alone for about an hour, and Nisa began to cry.

That night Nisa began to cry and I could not figure out how

to get up and get to her because if I used my crutches, how would I hold my baby? It took me I think thirty, maybe it was forty minutes, maybe it was less but I doubt it, to come up with an idea. I left the crutches alone and rolled off of my bed. Then I scooted on my ass across my room, down the hall, into Nisa's room. My leg was raised the whole while because that's what the doctors said I need to do in order to expedite healing, keep my leg raised one hundred percent of the time.

When I made it down the hall and then into Nisa's room, I pulled myself up using the crib as leverage. Then, with my free hand I reached into the crib and scooped up my baby, my baby who had withered into hysterics, since I'd taken so long. I picked her up with my one arm and lowered myself back down onto the floor with the other. And then we scooted back to my room, her on my good leg, the other leg raised. And I held her and rocked her and eventually, eventually she calmed down, she fell back to sleep, and so did I and the night was over, and honestly, I forgot about it.

I wouldn't be able to write about it now if weren't for my mother. She didn't forget about that night because it was she whom I called, panicked in the moment my baby had started crying and I couldn't figure out what to do to help her. I called my mom. And then, months on, it was my mother again who showed up, this time assuming the role of my memory. She reminded me in painful detail about what happened, how I'd been left, how Nisa had been. That's when I knew. What Nisa needed—including a strong, healthy mother—was always going to determine my final decision, even if it took me longer than I wanted it to for me to make that decision. Nisa was my choice.

Sometimes even now when Nisa feels as though it's just too hard to be a big girl, sometimes when she is just too tired and the day has been too long, and all she wants is for Mommy to pick her up and hold her, I do it. I do it even as big as she is because I remember when it was otherwise.

And years after, now when I think about that time and that man and when I think about the woman I was and the baby Nisa was, I still cry. Not all the time, but some of the time. I cry for the position I allowed myself to be in and I cry for all I gave away, not just my marriage, but my own heart, my own spirit. I cry for what that time, those years, had taken from my daughter.

I cry for the women I know who are still being taken apart by anger and violence. I cry for the women, for the children who will not survive it, who will never be able to offer an accounting of a night, let alone a lifetime, and I even cry for him. I cry to know how he lived with all of that rage, that seemingly immeasurable rage, when I know if things had been different, if he had had all he was supposed to have had, if his life had been honored in the way all of our lives deserve to be honored, then love would have been there inside of him, love would have been there instead and it would have crowded out the hate.

I cry for that lost possibility, not just in us but in and all around so many of us, the places where hate crowds out the love. But in my own life and at the end of that time, I had to not look at him and curse him nor curse the world. Instead I had to look at myself, at the woman I was, the woman I was not, and ask myself what I never wanted to ask myself, because who wants to realize that they're not the person they think they've already become?

I would have to ask myself this question, and find the heart to answer it:

Had I ever really loved myself? Had I ever handed myself over to myself, whole and complete, willing and wanting, the way I have with lovers, wide open and without barrier?

Ever once had I whispered into my own ear the words I had whispered to my lovers: there is no place I will not touch if it will please you, there is no place I will not love you?

Had I ever made the sacrifices, the financial ones, the ones physical, emotional, spiritual, and psychological, for my own edification like the ones I had made for him or for him or for him or for him?

I know I can claim the five, maybe six years of therapy off and on, on and off, hundreds of self-help books and articles torn from magazines, read and reread. I know all the prayers, all the calls to goddesses and gods, the pilgrimages to the waters, the forests, the confessional conversations, the revelations, the poems, but had anything worked either its magic or science and moved me closer to the place where I could claim my own heart, my own desires, and my own needs?

Did I ever commit to myself the way I did to others, and if I didn't, then why not? And if I didn't, is that why I found myself in my thirties still trying to stand, years after I could have sworn I had taught myself to run?

There was a time when I was in my twenties and even early thirties when I noticed myself, when I noticed where I was frayed and I sought to restitch those places, patch up. And to myself and to the world, my immediate world, the job I did to recast myself as a healthy whole woman was very convincing, even to me, especially to me. I looked in the mirror and reflected back a person who had shed vices, food, cigarettes, drugs. They had been replaced by love and a belief in a certain tomorrow with Rashid. There are witnesses who could tell you so.

Which is why it made no sense, why it sent me reeling the way it sent me reeling, when, as a mother, all I had put together so carefully started coming unwound, not unwound so much as chipped, broken off, small sections at first and then larger ones and then larger ones. Let me explain better.

I knew when I was pregnant I did not own my body. As a woman with a history of sexual abuse, not owning my body, not being in absolute control of it, should have been an unthinkable request for anyone to make of me. Except for my child, my baby. Not only with no hesitation, but with extreme pleasure, I allowed Nisa, even from the time before I knew she was Nisa, to direct the course, the details of my days. In fact, I reveled in it.

No longer did I push through exhaustion, nor show up in places out of obligation. I did what Nisa, communicating to me through every organ, through my bowels, my emotions, said for me to do.

A vegetarian for years, and more recently, pretty much a vegan, when I became pregnant, I ate roast beef at least twice at her demand, reintroduced chicken and fish as staples in my diet, lost my taste for sugar, and most bizarre of all, craved pears, a fruit I have held in particular disdain since I was a child. But my baby issued out these summonses on my lifestyle, my food choices, and without question I followed them and even enjoyed her dictates. I loved being pregnant. I trusted her orders.

And when my girl was born and I was the sole arbiter of the quality of her nourishment, we continued at this level of relationship, me quickly learning not to eat cabbage, hot sauce, and an array of other foods.

(After my less-than-successful start the night after she was born, when I chose pizza with fresh garlic and sun-dried tomatoes and Nisa cried for what seemed like eight hours straight from what I had transferred into my breast milk, I quickly went back to Cream of Wheat and built out from there—though slowly. Very slowly.)

In none of that time, not during the pregnancy, not during the near year I breast-fed, did I ever miss the parts of myself/my body/my life that I had handed over to Nisa. Perhaps I should have. Perhaps I should have been slightly more like girlfriends of mine who clamored to get back to owning their breasts, their diets.

A childhood of being trained how to give myself over to the whims of perverts, when I gave myself over for all the right reasons, I realized, albeit five years on, that I had little experience in taking myself back.

When people close to me asked, how after the good love that was Rashid, how could I fall in love with another man who could see me broken, hospitalized, I thought about the me as the baby who was given away moments after she was born and I thought about the child who was treated as a woman and I thought about the woman who, fifteen, eighteen years on, rushed to put all that behind her, but I hadn't. I hadn't. So that was how. Now I tell family and friends, just like that, and then I say I'm working hard, slowly, deliberately now to finish the work I began so long ago. But it doesn't happen overnight, despite all the meditation and prayers. It takes a very, very long time. Maybe it takes a lifetime.

the essence of a life in a day

*I*t's just past four and you are awake again. When was the last time you slept a whole night through? Maybe it's better, there's so much work you still have to do. You worry your editor won't like the story she asked you to crash in. You didn't really even want to take the assignment but you need the money. You'll turn in the story in just a few hours, pray your editor isn't a bitch about it. You need the money. You have no idea how you'll pay all the bills. Last month was flush. This month it's crazy. Nothing ever feels stable. Not money, not you. You, embarrassed you're going to have to ask your ex for a loan.

What kind of mother have you turned out to be? Close your eyes. Tell yourself to shut up and sleep for at least another hour. Tell yourself you cannot keep going without proper sleep. Pull the covers around you tightly, turn over on your side. Feel a push of heat between your legs. It's not sex you miss so much. You are not celibate. You miss being touched by someone who deeply loves you, and you know it. Love without question. Push the thoughts away. They will only make you angry. Think instead about your sister who still lives on the other side of the country. It's been a little while since the two of you have spoken. You miss her and tell yourself you'll call her later today.

Turn over to look at the girl cuddled up in a tight tiny ball right there beside you. Watch her breathe and feel yourself fall in love once again. A wave of joy spills over you. Stare at the girl, kiss her head, close your eyes. You really want one more hour of sleep. You have a long day ahead of you. Try to relax, you tell yourself this, but telling yourself this only makes you more uptight. Turn on the TV, some mindless bullshit ridiculous TV. Lie there but don't listen. Just think about your day.

What has to be done, how many different hats worn? Wish you could cry, pray for release, it doesn't come, they don't come, not one tear to say, Mommy, Mommy, anybody, anybody, I'm hurting, please help. Please. Instead you just wish, but wish without doing. Wish without the work it takes to make a wish come alive. But still you do it. Wish there was someone you could talk to right now. Then soon as you wish that, you tell yourself you're glad there's no one with you right now. You're sure you'd only sound like a whining, sniveling, ungrateful bitch. Hate the way you've become. Hate yourself so, so much.

Alarm goes off, you stare at it incredulous. How did two hours pass, how did you lose the time? Where did it go, what thoughts captured you so? You can't remember which ones made the hours speed like seconds. And this would feel shocking, you'd dwell on it and dwell on it if wasn't for the fact that you have to wake the girl. Nudge her gently, whisper her name, say it's time to rise. She opens her eyes slowly and lets them drift toward your face. She looks like she's sleepy but then suddenly breaks into a mile wide smile and begins to giggle.

You knew this was coming. This is how she wakes nearly every single day. She is smiling and giggling and grabbing at you, wanting to cuddle, wanting to be close. You lie with her for a moment and now she's asking what we're doing today, what have you planned that's fun and exciting?

It's a school day, you remind her softly, no big adventures until the weekend comes. A tiny temper tantrum follows: I don't wanna go to school. I want to be just with you. You remind her of her friends. You remind her how much she loves to learn new things. You remind her that this weekend the two of you will be going to the Bronx Zoo on Saturday and a birthday party on Sunday.

There's much to look forward to, which briefly she accepts and then falls back on not wanting to go to school. You go back and forth with her and then put an end to it. There's too much to be done, no time for this debate. You tell her enough is enough. You sound like your mother and this makes you smile. Maybe you do, after all, come from somewhere. Maybe that means you're really headed somewhere. You raise your voice, Mommy-firmness is perfect: Nisa, let's go. She's mad at you now, but there's no time this morning to indulge that either. Besides, by the time you're outside and walking to catch a cab, she's already back to laughter and incessant talking. You marvel at her, wish you had her recuperative skills. What a gift you think, both the skills, but more, the girl.

Arrive at her pre-K, a small independently run Black school in central Brooklyn. You love what she learns here, the way she can talk about Martin Luther King and Harriet Tubman despite the fact that she's not yet four. You could do without the few teachers here who wrap their faces in bitterness and walk out into the world, walk into the school, frown at small children.

But much as you want to dislike those sisters, in so many ways, you are exactly like them. Your act is just better. You say good morning to one of those teachers. She grumbles back at you, but so what? Nisa's bounded toward the center of the schoolhouse, the play space where the children gather each morning before venturing off into their separate classrooms. She's already in the midst of dress-up with her four best friends, Zakiya, Justine, Aanisah, and Ciara.

You walk over to say good-bye to your daughter. She jumps on you and so do her friends. You're on your knees hugging four little girls.

The best part of your day is about to end and it isn't nine in the morning yet.

You leave, walk past the teacher with the furrowed brow and apparently permanent frown, and you remind yourself that there's nothing that says a teacher has to smile or be pleasant. Anyway, none of the other parents seem to mind and there's nothing that can or even should, you suppose, mandate courtesy.

Still you wish people were kinder to one another, kind as a way of being, not as a single act and then it's all back to frowns and push-ing. You notice, as you're having that thought while walking away from the school and down toward the train station, that the only people who are "friendly" or "pleasant" to you are the men leering vulgarly from doorways and storefronts.

Arrive at work. Edit a story, write another. Take a break. Smoke a cigarette downstairs and hope nobody sees you. You feel so stupid, smoking cigarettes again. There's an editorial meeting shortly. Time to present your ideas for interesting stories. Tell yourself to remem-ber to keep your passion backed down. Your boss has used that word against you, passion as a curse, as something to be overcome.

And while passion is the word she uses, crazy is the word she means. You can tell by the way she always stares at you when you speak, with *that perplexed look on her face, her head cocked to the side. It's the same way you see her look at her own daughter, whom she speaks of terribly, so you can only imagine what she thinks of you.*

But whatever. This is your work, the reason the bills get paid, why your daughter is insured. You do the meeting with the best possible energy you can possibly summon and then afterward, you turn in an article you've just written. Make no mistakes. At least not today. No room for error today or any day. Not now that you're a mother. This is what you tell yourself and somehow really believe.

Take a break. Laugh with friends. Talk about your boss, how all of you wonder why she's still there. Agree to go for drinks this Friday coming, a much overdue girls' night out.

The day is over, you're back on the train. Crowded, stinking, alternately speeding and sputtering toward your Brooklyn station. Close your eyes. Try to relax, which once again makes you more uptight. Think about Rashid. Feel your throat tighten up.

Let him go, don't think about him.

Let him go, don't think about him.

Let him go, don't think, don't think don't think.

Push away the memories that are fighting for placement in the center of your brain. You flash to the feeling of lying in his arms, even if it was in a prison visiting room. Flash to the day Nisa was born, how you loved him then, how you had so much hope. Flash to what it feels like when he slides inside of you. Flash, go flush, cross your legs tightly, then

Stop.

You don't want to remember. You don't want to feel. You can end these crazy thoughts that do no one any good. Let the past be the past. Let the dead be with the dead. You tell yourself this over and over, but can't quite convince yourself, knowing as you do that time is unknowable, that there's no such thing as past, present, and future. There are no dividing lines in the fourth dimension. In the place where time lives and takes on shape and meaning to us, everything is in simultaneous existence.

Which is, you wonder, why it seems to come back in waves, a single, terrible question that hangs over each day, no matter what, it sits there: Did we ever really love each other? Has my whole life been a lie, were we a lie? What was true, the honest and entire space of desire? Did we ever really meet the way I told people we'd meet, in the full presence of ourselves and at the edge of our own nightmares?

Did we meet there despite our fears and did we take each other's hand and then make a stealthy escape? Have I ever once been honest? Me the girl with no traceable past, no root, no source? Am I even capable of it?

Wonder this every day. Each night on a crowded train.

Wonder if you ever really had the courage to dare all of the mean real-world enforcers, the enemies of light, the dastardly, the villains, to come do their best? Did you say they could not break you? And was that the problem? Your arrogance about the love you thought you'd shored up, the strong woman you thought you'd invented. Is that why she's gone and is this the penalty? These moments when you cannot remember, even as the train alternately speeds and crawls to your Brooklyn neighborhood, where you will see your girl, your girl with the face like her father's face. Beyond the love you have for that girl, you could almost be convinced, it doesn't exist. Love or safety or warmth. Romantic folly, perhaps. But not that other thing, the one that sustains people, couples across decades.

Think only about anger. This is what you live in now. The woman who shoves you on the train. The nasty store clerk who snaps at everyone. The terrible calls and e-mails you still get, two were even death threats from people who hated the book you wrote about loving Nisa's father. Think: I just want to be home. Want a cigarette, want a drink. Come on train. Hurry. Hurry.

Feel guilty. You should be thinking about Nisa. Nisa who asked just the other day about her father, about your marriage, about her own beginnings. You tell her she was created from a defining love, one that transformed, one that had the courage to honor its own dreams. She believes you, but do you?

You see pictures, letters, boxes and boxes and boxes of letters and cards, all detailing your old life. But you feel nothing, even with this record, you cannot find the place in your body, the place in your blood and in your brain that stores memory of this truth. Nisa deserves more. She deserves to know the arc of immeasurable romance that can exist in the world, in a life, so that she will be ready one day.

This is what you think about most nights as you ride that over-crowded train home each night. You think about it until you put the key into the lock and know you have to shake it off, at least act as if you have. Walk through your front door, get charged at by the girl. No one ever looks as happy to see a person as she seems to be every night when you come through the door. You hold her, you embrace her, you kiss her and snuggle. But something is missing and you can sense it quite deeply. The meditation you did when you got off the train, the one where you chanted and chanted, Don't feel anything, don't feel a thing, has cruelly carried over into areas where you do want to feel, but now it's too late.

You are holding your girl, you are smiling at her, but somehow you know that you are not really there. You're not really anywhere, truth be told. You start thinking again about how much you hate yourself. How this child with laughter for a heart, deserves better than you. You kiss Nisa and hug her and ask about her day. She rattles off a range of activities and observations and brand-new facts, none of which would make complete sense to any adult, but no matter. Her excitement translates and you love her for this, for her eyes and her heart, both so very wide open.

She has eaten now, she's bathed, and you bury your face in her tummy, fresh and clean as it is with that baby smell you love so much. You tuck your girl into bed and read her a story. She wants you to stay with her, to hold her through the night. You hold her for a moment and then you kiss her again. It's Mommy Time, you say to her, and she must go to sleep. You walk out of the room, hear her whimper in the background.

Pour a glass of wine, curl up on the couch. Call that mean boyfriend despite the rockiness of your relationship. The wine has made you loose. You want to flirt. And yes, okay, you want to feel loved. He's cold to you, says he couldn't reach you last night, and why didn't you call him all day long? You remind him that you'd said you had to report a story, file it right away. You've been swamped, you say earnestly, even if a bit defensively.

You start thinking again about how much you hate yourself. He's already broken your foot! Why argue? Why didn't you just make that goddamn call? This is what you think, but you do not say. You fight back when he gets like this now. Anything to retain a sense of dignity.

The argument descends into a full-blown screaming match with this boyfriend you claim, but who barely claims you. He says you are untrustworthy, you are a risk to the heart. You do not respond to this accusation anymore. You think your actions should speak for themselves, and besides, his constant refrain has gotten dull at this point. He accuses now, attacks, and instead of crying and defending, as you did for so long, you just think you hate him.

Which of course is not true. How could it be true if you keep going back to him, keep going back to the place where it hurts so bad?

Could it be really, really the case that any hate you feel is only ever about you?

Even when you have the right to be legitimately angry with someone else—someone like him—is the truth of the matter that your anger at yourself is the real problem?

You're wondering this while he is still spewing nastily about how you're a cheater. Despite your fear of his temper, you demand: How dare he speak to you like this when it's known by all how much he's out there fucking?

There, you said it. The thing between you that was not supposed to be spoken. It's the mirror before you both that no one wants to look upon. If he looks within, he is forced to see a man other than the one he wishes to present to the world—a man who lies, misrepresents, who manipulates, who hurts.

And you too, you have to see what the mirror shows you: a woman who, despite what she knows, what she's been privileged to experience, dumbs herself down, sets her own self up for so much of the hurt she lives. A woman who is not living the theory she believes.

You slam down the phone and pour another glass of wine. Drink it fast, pour another. Go to the bathroom. Smoke a cigarette out of the window. You cry a little, but not enough to get it all out. And it does cross your mind that it's crazy how you've gone from a relation-ship in which you were listened to, honored, respected, and loved, to this, to this, this entanglement that seesaws between high romance and abuse. The romance took you in, the romance you first felt with him, the dinners, the fine wines, the clubs, the walks through the thick sexiness that New York City nights can offer a couple. Yes, the romance took you in, but how is it that abuse is keeping you there?

You let these and other difficult questions go. You head back to the couch, turn on the TV.

The phone rings again. You are embarrassed that you hope it's him calling back, him calling to apologize, calling to make all things right with the world. At least all things right within the world the two of you inhabit. And while this has never happened once in all the times the two of you fought, for some bizarre reason, you still hold out hope. But hope for what?

This is the truth.

He was always content to let it all go, not look back. It was you who has spent the relationship running behind him. You check the caller ID. No surprise, it's not him. It's your girlfriend. You pause before taking it. She's always so angry. Even when she's laughing, joking around, she's using her words like weapons. You take the call but wonder why. Why the mean lover, why the mean friend? When did your life take such a shift that suddenly the people who are clos-est to you are also the people who are mean as shit?

That was never your story, never your life.

Is this some form of self-flagellation for leaving Rashid?

And if it is, why now, why beat yourself now when you're a mother, now when it's all the more important that those in your circle are loving and supportive, not demeaning and hurtful?

Their hurtfulness has a reach far beyond you. It can reach your daughter. You are painfully aware of this even as it occurs to you that despite the harshness of the people around you, maybe they're around you because somehow you think that their presence is better than being alone in the world. Better than not being seen at all.

You pick up the telephone, pour another drink. The wine is in your brain now. You feel warm all over and lie down on the couch as you begin the call. Your eyes are heavy, your thoughts are not. This is the state you have been wanting to achieve. To be here and to not be here at the very same time. It occurs to you that maybe you're trying to wish yourself into being some kind of pod person. But you dismiss the thought, enjoy the wine weaving through your brain.

You chat about nothing with your girlfriend and you breathe a sigh of relief when she has another call to take. You think: we made it through the conversation with no conflict or hurt feelings. Thank God, because you just couldn't take another fight tonight. But still the fear of it has kind of fucked with your high and you get off the phone and curse the path you've allowed your life to take.

You can feel the depression taking over your body. It starts as a threat that becomes a judgment that becomes a sentence that becomes a noose that morphs into a body bag that is slowly being zipped up over your face.

This is stupid, you think. It's ridiculous, it's selfish, it's wrong-headed and indulgent. What the hell do you have to be depressed about?

You with the incredible and enchanted girl.

You who gets paid to travel far and wide to beautiful places where "they don't speak English and don't even want to."

You who enters rarefied spaces.

You who have known great love.

You have no right to this nonsense, this sadness.

Pour a drink. Pour another. Stumble to bed. Look at the girl asleep and beautiful. Let the tears that spring to your eyes fall on your pillow. She is an entire universe to you and you think you are failing her. You think you are a failure. An image of Rashid flashes before you and then you pass out. Pass out cold.

Now it's just past four and you're awake again. When was the last time you slept a whole night through? Maybe it's better. Who can sleep when there's so much work that has to be done?

You worry your editor won't like the story she asked you to crash in. You didn't really even want to take the assignment but you need the money. You'll turn in the story in just a few hours, pray your editor isn't a bitch about it. You need the money. You have no idea how you'll pay all the bills. Money is so tight. Money is always so tight. Embarrassed you're going to have to ask your ex for a loan. Embarrassed because you keep winding up here, hand out and begging. What kind of mother have you turned out to be?

the new normal

Depression is a slow-moving illness. It takes hold but not all at once. It moves in on different parts of you, taking a piece at a time, and then what was a single day of feeling bad becomes a month, a month becomes a year. And a year, well after a year like this, the year becomes your new normal. At some point, it no longer seems strange to wake up each day and wonder how you will get through the first hour, the second. In the beginning it was wine every night and cigarettes that were my morphine.

Eventually it was sleep. I could barely get out of bed, see friends. Weekends would roll in and I would summon what felt like the heavens, every god, to make a life for Nisa. I did sleep-overs and trips to museums, Coney Island, the beach with my daughter and all her friends. My neighbors called my home, still call my home, Camp asha. "All the kids want to be with you," I heard over and over. And I suppose that had, in flashes, some truth, but it wasn't my big truth. Depression was. A huge abiding sense that I would never again have a life defined by love, by peace. That's where that thing takes you, how it leaves you, and in the end I was unable to do anything but the very basics to make a life work. I went into what I can only describe as hiding. In my room, under my covers, rising only to make breakfast or dinner. Rising when I could not avoid doing otherwise.

But I wanted more. I did. The desire for more was small at first, a cut below a whisper lost someplace inside me but I heard it, amplified as it became by my daughter's opposite way of engaging the world. Two years or more had passed and then one morning I looked at Nisa, the child who is so different than me, the child who knows her history, her roots, the child who never stays sad, who said to me once about a mean kid in her class, "I don't hold grudges, Mommy. I don't like to be angry and I don't like to be sad. You don't like being sad, do you?" her child logic outweighing my grown-up convictions.

I looked at her and saw for the first time in far too long what the universe has given me. This girl, this child who was not one in a million, but one of two point four million, to be exact. That's the number, that's how many of our babies are out here, trying to figure out how to navigate the world, while one of their parents, sometimes both of their parents, are incarcerated in this nation that locks up more people than any other on the planet. My daughter, not one in a million. My daughter, one of two point four million. And despite that reality, the faraway Daddy, the sad Mommy, she refuses to allow what she doesn't have to overwhelm what she does. She has always been loved and safe and warm. She has always been loved. She has always loved herself.

I sat up that day. Literally shook myself awake. "Come on, baby," I said that Friday morning. "We're playing hooky today.

From work, from school. We're just going to have fun." And we did. Movies, manicures, pizza for dinner. We had fun that day, and that day that was a beginning.

〜⌒

I DON'T HAVE MIRRORS all over my house. Mirrors are too hard now. There are none in my bedroom, no full-length looking glasses as there were in the days of my far more vain, or perhaps confident, twenties. There is one on the blue-and-white dresser that matches the little loft bed in Nisa's room. But that one is hers and I almost never use it. And then out from my bedroom painted orange and down the hallway painted lavender, there on the left is the bathroom sponged in forest green with marble floors to match. Inside there and halfway up the wall on one side of the room is a mirror that runs from nearly the door to the window. It was here when I moved in, though I've always said that had I been given the choice I wouldn't have put it up myself. Whatever the reason I first proclaimed that, now I know why. Now when I look at myself in that long, you-can't-avoid-it mirror, I see a face that is at once familiar and not, but still, I know it's me. This was not always the case and there came a morning when I knew it.

When I realized I had come undone—and that alone takes a moment—but when I realized I had come undone, my inclination was to stand in front of that mirror I hate and seek out myself. Where was that girl, that woman I once knew so well, the one who had shed all vice except for, of course, the need to not have any vice? Where was the woman who laughed? I would stare at the face that was in flashes a stranger's face and try to figure out where my own brand of crazy started, and it felt as though there was no beginning, only the possibility of an end and if I was going to get to an end, I had to tell the truth.

I had to have it make sense in my own head before it could make sense out loud. The terrible tangle of thoughts that wrapped around my brain, they were like drunken rants, disconnected, logic tossed aside, in pieces on the ground, sort of like me. This is to say, I had to stop lying. I had to take apart the story I had created and told others, but mostly I had to take apart what I had told myself.

I'd told myself, and later I told lovers, that I could leave my husband, my husband who in so many ways was real only to me anyway, my husband who existed for others only in Polaroid pictures or in the pages of a book. I told myself that I could leave that man, that marriage, and leave unscathed. I was not unscathed. No one gets out of a marriage, a good one, a bad one, unscathed.

I told myself I could not be undone by pain, me a hard-ass girl living in central Brooklyn. Not a place for the faint of heart, people from around here used to say. Besides, didn't I live a charmed life? Didn't I write celebrity stories, travel stories, books? I mean, yeah, I would say when I was pushed, of course it's sad about the marriage, really it is, but look on the bright side. There is so much good that's going on for me. I'm allowed to be grateful. Ask anyone spiritual: just be grateful. I want to be spiritual, recognize the gifts. Forget my silly little, probably patriarchal dream of an intact family, a house, a dog. I told myself that.

I told myself if I cried I was setting a bad example for my daughter. Others told me the very same thing. Told me never to be a victim, Black women are not victims and we are not weak. Tossed aside is Michelle Wallace's brilliant feminist tome about why Black women have always been, but should never have been, asked to be superwomen. In the post-welfare-reform days of the alpha mom, I was clear that being a victim, showing any weakness, was punishable by complete isolation and total loss of respect.

I was a mother, a single mother, a single Black mother. I was part of a tradition of women who do not bend and who do not break. This is what I said, this is how I now defined myself. As someone with no room for error.

And though in moments I did wonder if we really were all so strong, if nothing could break us. Where did I fit in among those Black mothers I see in the street, the ones who are screaming at their kids to shut up, shut up, shut the fuck up? In moments I wondered that maybe some of us who appear to have the charmed lives, the VIP thing going on, are not so far removed from the mothers who are losing it out there on the street.

And at times I wondered, Were we all one and the same kind of woman—the ones with the lips gone black from the pipe, stinking, messy, mad women, and the ones like me who have better cover? Were we the same? Did the difference really just come down to the quality of makeup we wear, the drug we choose? Did the difference just come down to the thirty-five-dollar tubes of Chanel lipstick, foundation mixed to exactly match your skin, and high-priced weaves you have to get real, real close to in order to notice that the whole shit is fake. But how often does anyone get really, really close? I wondered all those things and I wondered too, Was even I capable of getting close to myself?

And in the brief seconds I had the courage to consider these ideas, it occurred to me that maybe the fake thing is also part of the tradition, the mythical legacy of bravely forging alone in the wilderness that is single parenting and despite it all, emerging triumphant. That too is fake. That too is a lie. But are lies our heritage? Is our heritage something made-up, something fraudulent?

Because in the end, what is triumph? Where does the bar get set for Black girls and their babies? If we manage to have our children circumnavigate prison, does it make us winners? If we show up to church most Sundays even if we show up carrying two hundred extra pounds, diabetes, and heart disease? Are we winners then? If we shine as employee of the month, even if that shine is fueled by alcohol or drugs? What's the goddamn bar of triumph for Black girls and their babies? But when I think about that, it feels like way too much, so I tell myself it's all nonsense. I tell myself that these new thoughts, not my others, are the random drunken thoughts.

The clear thoughts, the ones that make sense are the ones that come with the television commercials for the quick-get-your-life-back fixes. This drug or that, take it and you're happy again, grinning or else running through a field made of green, unless, of course, you develop liver or heart or kidney disease. And if I can't get the drug, white wine will do. White wine was the truth. It did make me feel better. It did, I swear.

It took away everything that hurt. After a time, I couldn't feel my heart. My emotions were turned down, I was turned down, disconnected from myself. I said this was a good thing and I called my anger, pain, and sorrow by other names and I used Band-Aids in the place of body casts, and I told myself and I told everyone who listened, I was fine, just fine. I told myself that in no way, shape, or form was I anything like those scream-ing, cursing mothers. And I was right.

I did not scream or curse at my child. I would just say to her that I needed Mommy time and then I disappeared into one, two, four glasses of wine. I disappeared in that easy, kind of comfortable way that everyone can deal with because the bills are being paid and the deadlines are being met and the friends are being advised and the child is getting to school on time, looking cute and fresh in her brand-new clothes. I disap-peared and no one noticed, and even I didn't notice. I didn't notice until just before that day in front of the mirror, the mirror in the bathroom down the hall from the bedroom. The mirror I never wanted.

But before that morning in front of the mirror, there was a night. It was a night like one hundred nights before it, except there is something that inserts itself into my routine of wine and cigarettes. It is a small voice but it is a voice so clear. And there is no denying the truth of it. It touches me in a long-ago place, a time when my voice was that small and I was afraid to use it because I was afraid, because I am still afraid, at any minute I will be given back—so don't speak, don't make anyone angry, don't get in the way. This small voice on this average night is not afraid to assert itself. That is the truth. And I cannot ignore it. That is the truth. That small voice asking a question that embodies the truth:

Mommy.

Mommy.

Where are you?

Are you here?

Are you here and are you with me, Mommy?

Mommy?

dreams

This is the hour I live for. This is the hour I live. I am here in the hushed dark and I am watching my daughter sleep. I am watching her deep, full breathing, her arms outstretched, her face wearing the look of peace and content. And her face, the one I can stare at and lose myself in, I lose myself in the smooth and round and beauty of her face, buried and breathing now into my breast.

The day has been long, it has felt impossible, it's felt immeasurable, but it was not and we are here, survivors on an aching planet; both us and the planet, both of us, are still pulsing with life. And in this hour and in this moment, with work and school and plans and lists, and everything, everything that was to be done, actually done, we are here, and we are together and we are at peace.

And peace is what I always feel when I am with her, with Nisa, the clown, the freely affectionate, the lover of strawberries, sushi, spaghetti, and ginger ale (though not in that order).

Nisa, whose sense of joy and mischief could be marketed.

Nisa, who is silly and bossy and demanding, although she does work very, very hard at sharing. She really, really tries.

Nisa, my little Aries, my fire sign who spits fire, born as she was in the Year of the Dragon.

Nisa, my team member, my cheerleader, my baby who said when she was three years old and I was feeling fat or ugly or probably both, "But you're a beautiful African queen, Mommy."

Her, that girl. The one who, looking at my mostly bargain-store shoe collection one day, announced very definitively that she only liked the "Finolos" (apologies to Blahnik—but she was just four at the time).

Nisa, who, on a seventy-five-degree September evening, threw on her fresh, newly handed-down shearling and when we suggested maybe it was a little warm outside for the coat, she looked at everyone as if they were crazy and replied, "But I have to work it!" which is when she broke into a walk that would have turned even Naomi Campbell's head.

Nisa, my self-defined abstract artist and singer in the tradition of Beyoncé, Nina Simone, Hannah Montana, and the Cheetah Girls, depending on the day, depending on her mood.

Nisa, who loves cotton candy, cucumbers, Coney Island, and being from Brooklyn.

Nisa, who wants a dog and who does not understand "lease provisions." Her, that girl.

She is never my problem, never the struggle, never the one who disturbs my peace. I tell people that when they offer assistance, offer to watch her for an hour or two. She is not my problem. She is my joy.

People say, and I believe them, How can I help? I say nothing. It's not that there isn't any help I can use. But who would I or who should I turn to when my stress is born of a sudden forty percent increase in the cost of my rent and no concurrent increase in my income level?

Who can hold me down if the bottom line is this: I need to work outside the home just a little bit less so that I can make dinner for my daughter just a little bit more?

Who I am supposed to call about needing a health-care system that doesn't take days to navigate and that considers mental health issues real and a priority? Or a health-care system that was just affordable and accessible? If someone wants to make me an offer, then be warned: these are the things I could really use help with. There are times I have really needed a human being and not a computer that leads to nowhere on the end of whatever customer-service call I'm making. But if not that, then perhaps a public education system that doesn't take a one-size-fits-all approach to teaching children or operate on a fear-based discipline theory even when those whom they're scaring are people who are five and six years old, seven and eight and nine years old.

I would like a nation of schoolhouses that actually look like schoolhouses and not detention centers where even now, today, too many first graders are walking into their schools and their initial encounter is with cops and sometimes metal detectors, and so in case those children didn't know it before, they know by the time they've walked through years of detectors, been watched by years of police officers, seen years of bars on windows, that whatever anyone told them, dreamed for them, they know their real destiny in this world is to one day be a prisoner. I could use that change.

I could use a country where no child really ever did get left behind. I could use an end to the war in Iraq, the conscription of children into armies, the genocide in Darfur, and the persecution of women in Afghanistan. I could use police who cared about my well-

being and the well-being of my child and the well-being of children of mothers I know and I do not know. I could use a police force who didn't have a habit of shooting unarmed Black men or women or kids. Fourteen-month-old kids. I could use a grocery store in my neighborhood that sold organic foods. I could certainly have used a different response to Hurricane Katrina.

I could use a media that reflected in relatively real time the world it claims to cover. I could use a little more courtesy when I'm out in public. I could use far less concrete. I could use having my daughter's father home from prison. I could use having many fathers and mothers home from prison.

I could use an end to child abuse and rape and sexual harassment and male domination and white supremacy and all the isms that keep us hobbled and hurting.

They disturb my peace, those things do, but not her. Never my Nisa.

Even on the days when I have sat there just stunned watching her, Nisa, launch into a third straight hour of talking, of jabbering, on and on about absolutely nothing, but the sound of her own voice delights her even if it does make my eyes water up and cross. Even on those days, those endlessly noisy, exasperating days, she does not disturb my peace.

If I have any peace at all it is because of those days and these nights. And this is what I'm thinking as I stroke her hair lightly and watch her as she sleeps, and then without warning her small body jumps. She jerks in her sleep and I am suddenly afraid, my fears are so constant, so present, even in this hour when I think I've banished all the negatives away.

Put to the test, I go right there: something terrible must be happening inside of Nisa's head and I am waking her gently but urgently from the nightmare that I'm certain has gripped her sleep, because too often they have gripped my sleep, and before I can remind myself she is not me, my experiences have not been Nisa's experiences and they will not be, she may never have nightmares, before I can tell myself any of that, I am calling her name, I am whispering it into her ear, Nisa, Nisa baby, wake up, wake up.

I am asking her this as her eyes open slightly, then shut again tightly. Nisa baby, what are you dreaming, what are seeing when you close your eyes? Are there monsters, is something wrong, you jumped in your sleep. And she pauses before she answers, this child who is still free, and I swear I do not want to put my stuff on her, my hurt, and I curse myself for having just done it again and I make another silent promise that I will stop. I will stop right now. And as I am making this promise with my arms around my child, Nisa says to me quietly but deliberately and just like this: I'm dreaming of rainbows, Mommy. Go back to sleep.

reasons to live

W hen I at last had the courage to really look at myself, my errors, it finally dawned on me that yes, of course I would stop eating properly.

Of course I would start smoking again.

Or drink every night.

Or have unhealthy relationships, both romantic and platonic.

Of course I would alienate the people closest to me.

In the most simple terms, depression is a broken heart. And if the heart is not working, not pumping the blood, nothing else works either.

So then of course I would feel guilty. Who would imagine, after all my rhetoric, that this was the kind of role model any child should have? Certainly not me. What kind of future was I ushering in for her?

The cliché is that children have as much to teach us as we do them. And like most clichés, those words rang empty to me until I lived them. I lived them all the way out. And now I know that they are true. There were times in the midst of my great sadness when I would confess to friends the terrible breadth of the sorrow that had this viselike grip on my neck, my heart.

I cannot count the number of times people would say to me to look at Nisa and just live for her. Wasn't my daughter enough? I was asked more times than I care to recall. Far, far more times.

I hated those admonitions because on the other side of them was the notion, the idea, that somehow I did not love my daughter with the whole of my heart. But I knew that the key was and would always be in me rediscovering the value of my own life, the measure of my own worth. I just didn't know where to find that key and if I did find it, would I also find the lock it fit?

Yet, when I was able to shut out the world, the world beyond Nisa, and I just watched the way my daughter moved through life, I thought I might find the key, that it wasn't hidden so well that it would remain forever beyond reach. If only I could have stayed in those moments, the ones that leave you in joyous disbelief: did my five-year-old child really just wander through the Basquiat exhibit, turn her nose up, and grunt, "This isn't so great, Mommy. I can do better." And then do it?

Did I really come home the next day to Nisa proudly displaying a painting, and with a big ole *I told you so* attitude, and then demanding that I take it to the museum and have it hung? Did she really say to me the next day, after I told her I showed my friends her work, did she really, with arm gestures and all, at five years old, say to me, "Oh, Mom! Now everybody's gonna crowd me up!"

Nisa, my reluctant celebrity, my modern-day Greta Garbo.

And Nisa, my baby who takes my two rules—safety and manners—so much to heart that she will charge anyone who curses in her presence a dollar. For every curse. Curse more than twice, she's negotiating for punitive damages. And no one is safe, not even people who don't curse, because she adds other words to the list of "bad words." She's charged people for using the terms "shut up," or "ugly." "They're not nice" or "appropriate," she'll snort as she demands payment from you.

We curl up in bed sometimes and watch reality shows—she loves them—but none more perhaps than *Project Runway*. At some point, she pulls away from me, leans closer to the television, crosses her arms, and begins doing her running commentary. It would drive me—probably almost anyone—bananas if she didn't make the very same calls the judges make, *each time*. And I think, this is my girl, mine?

I like nice clothes as much as the next person, but surely I can live a year in gym clothes if given the opportunity, if given a year without public appearances or dinners. How did I end up with Anna Wintour's secret love child?

But still, my Nisa, a child like so many others, rejects categorization. Her inner fashionista is not held back by the girl she is in school, the one who loves math and technology and reading and art. And while she loves figuring out math problems, even, God help me, word problems, it doesn't mean that she won't break free from me as soon as we enter the playground, calling over her shoulder that's she's going to make a friend.

From a safe distance I watch her, I listen. She will approach a child of her approximate size and ask, "Want to be friends?" Nothing holds her back from being just who she is: a little girl.

My daughter sees the potential for fun everywhere and tells me so. Not in those words of course, but in her daily excitement at simply this: we are alive and we are here and there are worlds out there that need discovery. Every weekend offers another opportunity, and try as I might to get her to allow me to sleep past six-thirty or seven, she will say, "I just can't help it, Mommy," and she will mean it.

She, more than anything, has been life-saving for me. I look at her and think of the baby I was who was given away and I think about the girl I was who was spirited away and I know that I am a woman now, able to see what it might have been like, to have been loved from the beginning, to have been wanted from the beginning. It's doesn't fix everything, this sort of vicarious way of healing. But it does help.

When I have believed that what I wanted more than anything else was to fold into my depression, stay in bed, not eat, not shower, not speak, move only enough to deal with the essentials, Nisa reminded me that the essentials include a walk in the park, spending time with friends, having dinner together. At the Botanic Garden just down the road from our Brooklyn home, when we go to see the roses each spring as they come into bloom, she literally makes us stop so we can smell each one.

It was Nisa who got me to finally take a walk in the woods once more, stand beneath the redwoods and gasp as we looked up and up but could not find the top of them. It was Nisa who returned the wonder of butterflies, the carousel, the majesty of the ocean, the beauty of an ancient shoreline.

She notices babies, dogs, the color of autumn's falling leaves.

She tries to wrap her arms around the wind.

She sees life all around her and wants to embrace it at every turn.

And she wants me to be there too, full of excitement and embrace. That my daughter is all the way present in her life allows me to think, in my more clear moments, that I can do it too. I can be all the way present, if Nisa is to be believed. I did it before, there is a record of this, and I want it back, the feeling of being all the way in my own life. I want it now. Especially now.

How can her joy not be a cure-all, a magic bullet, an impenetrable shield against the sadness? In at last paying attention to this, paying attention to it more than to the frustrations, the harshness that can puncture all of our lives, each day stopped seeming as though it was just something to get through rather than something to live in.

And I don't want or mean to sound Pollyannaish. Like any mother worthy of the title, I have lost my temper with Nisa, responding to her dramatics with my own. I have never hit anyone and could never imagine hitting my own child—but, let me tell you, I was a world-class yeller.

But the longer I was a mother, the longer we did this thing together, the clearer it became that most of my annoyances, most of what sent me off into the land of the banshee, were mostly to do with all the many things that pull and prick at us. Kids can annoy you with the constant questioning or talking (I read somewhere that the average four-year-old, clutch your pearls, asks 429 questions a day). But for most of us who are lucky enough to only have to negotiate the usual irritations— bedtime, homework and such—the thing that sends us out of ourselves is usually never just the kid. It's the child and the bills and the partner or no partner and the housework and the idiot boss and the three percent raise against six percent inflation and the wacko driver who cuts you off and almost kills you. It's all those things or some of those things added up together with the

429-questions-asking cutie-pie you really do love but God please, just be quiet, please baby, please. Though please baby please is often not the first way it comes out of your mouth. What comes out are like those serpents and rats from our childhood poems. It comes out mean and it comes out loud and what I finally came to understand was that it didn't work. If my goal was to make life simpler, more calm, then yelling my way through it resolved exactly nothing.

A teacher and friend told me once the best thing you can do in shark-infested waters (if you can't get right the hell out, of course), is to be still. So that has become my goal: to be still, to be calm, to focus more on what I do have rather than what I don't have. For sure I don't always manage it and even when I do, it doesn't always make things either feel or actually be better, but overall, I know I am not as continually sad at the very core of myself as I once was. And that's not only good news for me. It's also good news for my daughter, who, much to my surprise, looked at me one day recently and said, "Mommy, if I was gonna describe you, I would say you were calm. You're silly. But you're calm. And I like that a lot."

No one was in more shock than me to hear those words. And no one more than me wanted to be able to live up to that edict more, either.

So it was this conviction that was finally married to all of these amazing remembrances, the ones that came wandering back when I first started on my return. The conventional wisdom all these years on remains that if you're nervous because you have to speak in front of a crowd, picture the audience naked or else focus on that one friendly face in the crowd. Because I think so much of what my story is about is being nervous in front of life, I have my own trick. I picture Nisa. I picture her at all ages. I remember how even as a baby, the sight of her round knees, her cherubic cheeks, the sound of her fast raucous giggles, has always brought me immeasurable delight.

It changed me, those images of my baby, in the moments that spiraled into some unattractive version of frenzy, and in the middle of tears or their internal twin, I would demand of myself: why the hell can't I just settle into gratitude and even bliss? When I nearly became nauseous with guilt from that question, I would pretend that all I needed to feel better was to remember my child's face. And then one day it wasn't pretending anymore.

In my better moments, in my best moments, I know that what I have to do, what I have to learn, perhaps relearn, comes daily from the four-foot-and-a-half sage with whom I live, the one who instructs because she inhabits, rather than because she is inhibited by, all the corners of her life. She sees possibility and color and light in each corner of her life. She sees reasons to live. And what will I ever teach her that is greater than this lesson she offers freely to me?

But then it occurred to me the thing she doesn't know, the thing I want to show her. Renewal. Children, if life is fairly good to them, will not have to learn this while they are still small. Adults, if we live any measure of time and with any measure of energy, will most certainly run headlong into it, that challenge: to come back or not. Many of us will have to learn it over and over. We will have to figure out how to renew ourselves after the loss of a love or a job or a friend or a parent—or ourselves.

We figure it out or else we give up and then there is nothing to save, nothing to renew. I did not give up, not all the way, not even at my lowest points. I remember standing in the center of my own hell, and a close friend of mine reminded me, just like this she said it: *asha, you are a survivor.* And something switched on, a tiny beam of light. It was true. There was evidence. And one of those pieces of evidence was this girl, my daughter.

open wounds

When I began the process of excavation, trying to understand myself in a context that was both who I was and who I was a part of, I had to admit that this is the truth:

Sixty percent of Black women in the United States suffer from depression.

Forty-three percent of Black women in the United States report that they were verbally or emotionally abused during their childhood.

Forty-two percent report that they were sexually or physically abused during childhood.

Every single day in America, this big and wealthy nation of ours, somewhere there is a mother dying during childbirth, somewhere else there are four children who are being killed by abuse, five more who are committing suicide, another eight, still, dead from firearms, thirty-three from preventable accidents, still another seventy-seven who will not know their first birthdays.

The contributing factors for depression among Black women include sexism and racism but also economic insecurity. With more Black households headed by single mothers than not, we are at the top of the list of those at risk for depression and all its many symptoms.

And yet Black women are twice as unwilling as whites to seek mental-health treatment. We fear it. This is what we say. We are actually afraid of it. Indeed, we are more afraid of potentially getting well than we are of living in pain, living a half-life.

But this is also the truth, it's my truth.

I have been in therapy on and off since I was a teenager, most deliberately and intensely during my first years with Rashid when I was struggling to come to terms with the childhood sexual abuse. I don't wear this as a badge, and it is nothing I feel especially proud of. It's just how it was, *that's the truth,* whether or not I liked it, which I never have.

I have tolerated therapy because I had to. It is hard enough to face oneself, and harder still to do so with another person, a stranger listening in. Culturally, it argues against everything Black girls are raised to know and believe in. What we know, what we grow up knowing, is "Do not, do not, put your business in the street." Lying on someone's couch and telling them how it was in your mother's house or your husband's house or just how it is to live in your own head—well, it simply is not done.

Two years after the storms, I was in New Orleans participating in a workshop about depression and post-traumatic stress disorder, particularly but not exclusively in the wake of Hurricane Katrina. And sister after sister would come up to the microphone and speak of her life. And here I mean her life beyond, before, Hurricane Katrina hit. With each one, with each grown woman, we heard tale after tale of sexual assault, racist humiliations, missing fathers, murdered children, domestic violence.

At the end of the panel, after all questions had been asked, one of the women who worked in the venue approached the mike. She said she simply could not understand all this talk. She said she had survived Katrina despite enduring the inhumanity we saw night after night on the news in the days that followed August 29, 2005. She said she felt that, yes, yes, she had indeed lost it all, but finally she was coming back and she was coming back because of one thing we had not mentioned in the space: God. She said she didn't know why anyone would need therapy if they had God.

I am no doctor. Nor can I prescribe what can walk someone back into their soul after an experience or series of experiences have worked to wrest it away from them. But I remember thinking that this is the advice I heard growing up—Let go and let God (although my mother's line was, Pray like it all depends on Him, work like it all depends on you). She was not unfamiliar to me though, this sister.

I believe in prayer. I believe that prayer can create belief and belief can inform action. I will never let it go. Prayer and meditation have been my morning ritual for nearly all of my adult life. But the setting aside of other interventions scares me. I want us to pray and then call the doctor, and if there had been time on the panel that day, I would have said that to this sister. I would have said that and then I would have asked her what I finally asked myself: If a car hits you while you're crossing the street, and you go flying five feet in the air and then come crashing down and your legs are broken and your skull is cracked, would it be enough for me to pray, or should I pray while whipping out my cell phone and calling 911?

I would have told her that sometimes the car is not a car but a broken levee and the Ernest N. Morial Convention Center or else the Superdome and a president and government who leave you there to die. You and your babies and your mother and your husband and your brother and your sister and all of your cousins too.

Sometimes the car is not a car, but a grown-ass man whose hands can't keep themselves off a seven-year-old girl or boy. Or a fifteen- or sixteen-year-old girl or boy. Sometimes the car is a best-selling R & B singer.

Sometimes a car is not a car but a neighborhood cop who thinks every Black child they see has a bull's-eye on their back, but that child was your baby, your baby named Timothy Stansbury. Your baby who was committing no crime. Your baby who died young because he lived Black.

Sometimes a car is a husband or a lover or a brand-new acquaintance with a quick hand and a vulgar sense of entitlement.

Sometimes a car is the father who left you or the mother who never noticed you. Or who cursed you or slapped you into a small, hurt, mean little shell of yourself.

But whatever it is, a man, a president, a cop, a father, a mother, whatever or whoever it is, you still wind up hit. You still wind up five feet in the air. And after, the broken bones, the cracked skull, may not be the broken bones and cracked skull the way we know them to be.

Sometimes, the broken bones are the nightmares that come back and back down through the years, no matter how many years.

Sometimes a cracked skull is the same bad relationship you enter—romantically or platonically—again and again. The names change, the faces change, but the relationship is the same and constant and your skull has still been cracked and gone untreated.

And sometimes, sometimes what is broken and what is cracked can only be seen as a rage you cannot release no matter how beautiful the day: the sky is a nearly made-up blue, shining within the push of light; and also there is money in the bank account; and the bills are paid; and you receive a kind phone call from a friend you'd thought lost. But whatever the goodness, it is lost to you, and on any given morning that will become an afternoon and night, there is only anger. And you wear it, your anger, in blinding, brutal colors.

What it is, is the feeling you have every morning that nothing is quite right, although neither can you put your finger on what is wrong. Sometimes this is the case. Sometimes this is the only evidence of the broken bones.

Of course, sometimes the only evidence is Newport Lights. Or alcohol.

~~~~~

THERE CAME A MORNING when I was asked to help care for a friend who had come undone. We, his partner and I, had to rush him to the hospital. The danger presented at that moment was physical, but we knew that it was born of injuries we could not see, the mean loops in his brain. We'd seen him on rants and we'd seen him spiraling out, but before now there was no blood and so we just kept moving, kept telling ourselves it would all work out.

But before I could go and do whatever was in my power to try to help my friends, I had to drop my daughter off at her pre-K. Not just drop her off. I had to take time to sit with my Nisa, to sit with her friends.

I realized I needed them as much as they needed me as we

walked through the school door that early June morning. I knew
that before I could confront a spirit torn down, I needed to look
on these brand-new and emerging spirits, ones that were as yet
unknotted, unbroken at their core. I knew that in order for me
to withstand bearing witness to my friend, to the ever-widening
space of his anguish and the anguish his behaviors imposed on
those closest to him, I needed to be witness to who we all once
were, who we all might be again: honest beings, and all the way
in our humanity, all the way intact.

At Nisa's pre-K just then, when the beauty of the day belied
the ugliness of the reality I knew was happening in the life of
my friends not two miles away, I sat on the carpet with a small
grouping of children who were three to five years old. They
were children I had joyously been watching for two or three
years as they grew and changed.

They were children who at different moments I had listened to
as they expounded on the details of their life. But mostly when I
was with them, what they wanted was for me, Mama asha, to read
them a story, entertain them, make funny faces, use silly voices.

They did not ask for that though on that late spring morning. On that morning, for some reason, it was not books they
wanted me to read to them, nor was it the retelling of a story
they had pulled out of their dreaming and asserted as fact. It
was wounds that they were speaking of and five-year-old Ciara
was the one who set it off.

"Look at my boo-boo, Nisa-Mommy," she exclaimed, and
then directed me to a tiny, barely visible dot on her leg.

"There!" she yelled, triumphantly, and together we discussed
it. We ooohed and we aaahhed, me and the other children. I

furrowed my brow, expressed sympathy, but mostly I noted her bravery, her crazy, hard-core survival skills.

And that's when the rest of them joined in: a months'-old scab on an elbow from one, a tiny scratch on a knee from another. I showed them my foot, the one that had been shattered. I showed them the scars from the surgery. They were fascinated by all the marks and together we continued to ooohh and aaahh. Then they each shared the gory details of their playground war stories, each one leaving us all wide-eyed and rapt, our mouths agape.

By the time my Nisa—who refused, of course, to let anyone upstage her in front of her own mother—was finished telling the story of her wounds, they had taken on such huge, shocking, and really tragic proportions, I thought it was a wonder, a miracle from the Universe that she wasn't laid up somewhere in full traction. With a patch over her eye.

Still, in all of our makeshift show-and-tell, it occurs to me that there is comfort in wounds that can be seen, these tangible, irrefutable markers, these hurts, no matter how small, that can be pointed out, proven. Man, there is nothing like a tangible piece of evidence!

Evidence of being wounded—and I mean evidence that's the kind we can see, the kind that is familiar to us—is so much better than the more shadowy sort, the sort you have to squint at and get real close to see. What do we do with evidence that insists on hiding, that nests inside of some dark part of the brain that even the doctors, with all of their fancy instruments, theories, and drugs, cannot find? That's the bad kind of evidence, the kind you can dismiss. Yet for most of us who have ever been blown to the border, looked over the very edge of it, and then wondered—Could I go?—it is what we are left with.

My uncle, my mother's only brother, who was one of two children on a ward who survived a 1930s spinal meningitis outbreak, still lost much of his hearing. What I learned from my mom, what she learned watching him maneuver the world of the deaf, is that of all physical challenges, people who have lost their hearing get the least sympathy of all. We can see someone who is living with blindness or perhaps the inability to walk. But deafness does not jump out at us. In my uncle's case, he quit a better-paying, higher-ranking job that he had with an airline to be a janitor, because there, behind the broom, no one made fun of him, which is what had happened in his previous position. There is something about the wounds we can see. I am telling you this is true.

And on that morning, the children and I gleaned sympathetic eyes—however briefly—for the tragedy of our scars. And it helped, somehow. I saw it in the children's eyes and I felt it inside my own heart, the importance of this moment when our wounds were there, public and displayed. Our wounds, visible, and so our wounds, undeniable. Our wounds, acknowledged.

Months and months later when I returned to therapy, it was that morning and those children and my friends and our scars and all that I took from that experience that I was thinking about. And I said it to my doctor almost just like this:

I want my wounds acknowledged. I want them healed.

And I want myself back.

That's what we all have to say, at some point what we have to demand.

Give me back.

Give me back.

Chapter 13

coming back

This is what it came down to. I had to leave much of what I'd known, much of what had been my life, behind. The entertainment reporting, the fancy hotels, the semi-high-profile position, the parties, the people who said they loved me but really did not, the people who didn't say that they loved me and really, really didn't, I left them all behind. And I took a fellowship at Columbia University, and for a year I lived a very quiet life.

I went back to the gym and I wore only workout clothes for a year and sort of got back into shape and I went to no parties and hung out with very few people and spent nights reading to my daughter instead of drinking on the couch, and once during that time I saw a baby be born, and also, then, I wrote. I wrote and published another book of poems a year after I'd lurched toward this self-transformation, all the contents of which were about violence against women. Not that I was aware of this.

I realized it only after a reader pointed it out, and because I had not recognized it myself, the content of my own work, I could no longer ignore how removed I had been from the details of my own life, which is probably what made me do it, made me take the big step. I told a friend in a voice well above a whisper, I really need help.

I told her about the three years in the bottle and the violent relationship and the depression and the guilt and losing Rashid and losing my marriage and I told about the mean boss. I told everything and I told it without seeing myself as a woman who was violating some Black-girl rule.

I told it without the sense that I was, as someone once said to me, whining about "my tortured life" or embracing a "victimization motif." I told it without looking to self-flagellate, and, most important, I told it because I believe in bearing witness to our own lives and when I had not done that myself, I disappeared.

I did not want to be a disappeared person. And I told because Gloria Morrow, a psychologist who practices in Pomona, California, and whose patient roster is ninety percent Black women, said simply, "There's nothing worse than suffering in silence."

Morrow talks about the imposition of sexism and racism in our lives, how it plays out in our homes and in the workplace, and how both of these victimized, *yes, victimized*, us and finally we had to be able to say it. We had to say it even at the risk of being told to shut up, or stop complaining. We had to say it because not saying it, not facing it, was a direct route to anxiety and depression and all the ways each of these impacts our total well-being.

Given my choices, the self-defeating choices I made while grinning and meeting deadlines and pretending everything was fine when nothing was fine, I knew that she was right. So I told.

And then I went back to therapy.

My DOCTOR WAS THE real thing, a psychiatrist who did not just hand me some pills and send me on my way but was one who talked. A tall, imposing genius of a woman originally from Detroit, she was plain-spoken, and blunt, and she came to me at the recommendation of a dear friend. It's funny how life works, why I believe all time exists all at once. As it turned out, my doctor is also the first psychiatrist I ever saw, back when I was a sixteen-year-old student struggling at Howard University.

I can't remember how much time—one session, two—lapsed between my recounting of the last few years, the recounting of a lifetime, and her half looking at me, half pulling down one of her books to confirm what it seemed she already knew. She peered at me over her glasses, and directly, "Ms. bandele," she said, voice calm and sort of midwestern flat, "you have post-traumatic stress disorder."

Post-traumatic stress disorder? The war disease? The Vietnam legacy?

Yes, she said, but it doesn't affect only soldiers emerging from combat. It can impact anyone, she explained, who has lived through a traumatic and life-altering experience, one in which grave harm occurred or was threatened. Nearly eight million Americans suffer with it, albeit in varying degrees. And while symptoms of PTSD often show up within three months of an incident, often it can take years. It affects women more often than men and is characterized by a person who startles easily (check) or who abuses substances (check, check), emotionally distances themselves from people to whom they used to feel close (oh, God, Rashid, check, check, check).

For some, the condition is chronic. I was lucky. I was treatable.

I had access to treatment. For many of us, bent under the weight of either depression or its more intense relative, PTSD, there is nothing, no one to explain to us what we are dealing with, and explain that it may be the result of one thing or perhaps the result of many things. It may not be the childhood sexual assault, in other words, that sends you reeling headlong into the netherworlds of PTSD or depression. But that experience, that violence, retriggered by, say, a boyfriend who breaks you up, hospitalizes you two decades on, well, that can do it.

For me, for many, it was everything added up together. And none of it ever fully attended to. It is no different than if you have a broken leg and the bones don't get set quite right and afterward you keep falling, you keep reinjuring that leg. Each time you fall, the breaks, the hurts you endure, may not all be of the same severity, but taken as a whole, the result, the cumulative result, is devastating.

Still it was a big name, a big diagnosis. It sounded bigger than me, more important. I said this to her, that people who got this had lived through really horrible events. I talked about the men and women in Iraq, our soldiers, and also the Iraqi citizens trying to make a life in the middle of a war zone. "That's who's been through something for real, for real."

"Like survivors of abuse, Ms. bandele," she said, again in that matter-of-fact voice I came to rely on in the time we worked together. And just like that, there they were: my wounds, without recrimination, without minimizing, without excuse, simply acknowledged.

I would argue that that was when we really began to work.

We worked in ways I had never worked before with a doctor.

We worked until I was well enough to manage my own care. We worked for months that long winter into spring. We sat in my doctor's home office until we developed a clear plan about what to do going forward. We worked until I had no more money to afford the sessions and then she allowed me to barter with her—I did some editing for her—so that the work could continue.

We talked about why I needed to exercise and why I needed to stay engaged with my routine even on the days I most wanted to just sleep. We talked about strategies to help me sleep at night without any substances. Who knew that getting into bed with Nisa and reading stories with her at night was more relaxing than red wine? Who knew what I needed had been there beside me?

We talked about friends in my life whom I found hurtful. We talked about the right to release the people whose words and actions diminished me rather than strengthened me. She reminded me that I had no obligation to remain close to them. We talked about the right to say, No, a word that I, like so many women, struggle with.

"I feel bad if I let someone down," I said. "But you're letting yourself down," she reminded me. "Don't you count?"

She said guilt, as my mother has often said, is a useless emotion. We talked of shame, another corner of my depression, another part of myself that kept me from taking care of myself. Why take care of something you're ashamed of, even if that thing is the woman in the mirror? Shame is not positioned to help or heal anyone, though I know how we lean toward it, run toward it, wield it like a knife.

In the days before prison, long ago, on another continent, shame was the center point of punishment. An entire village might turn its back—physically—on an offender (or perceived offender). It was, in some places, the worst punishment one could receive. Of course too, we know it here, in the American system of jurisprudence: from the seventeenth-century stockades to the twenty-first-century perp walks, shame is still very much a part of who we are.

And in some ways it is effective. It can elicit an immediate response. The shamed one offers an ocean of tears, a head hung low, followed by a deeply passionate and public apology. But it does little to transform much in any lasting way. If it did, of course, we would not see the same people making the same mistakes over and over. Shame may stop a particular behavior in a given moment but it does not move a soul, and when you want to shift something in a person so that it doesn't shift right back, there is only one tool to use and that tool is love.

It is the only proven method, the one that lasts. Cruelty and fear and shame work only until those who have been cowed get their own weapons. I was no different. Feeling ashamed of my behavior, my self-berating, the berating by some of the people I pulled around me, did little to make me a stronger, clearer—sober—person.

And now I look realistically at the people of this nation, realistically at myself, and know addiction and self-abuse and self-destructive behaviors are as American as apple pie. We may excoriate some and not others, but all that acting out begins at the same source, in the same river of pain, of disconnection.

The National Institute on Drug Abuse reported in 2004 that some twenty percent of our population—48 million people—

have used prescription drugs for nonmedical reasons in their lifetime. And these are *licit* drugs! Not coke or weed or meth or dope but the stuff that is in our parents' medicine cabinets. But for just the prescription stuff alone, 48 million! What, then, are the numbers when we consider all those who struggle with health and other issues, because from McDonald's to meth, from Vicodin to Valium, from weed to wine, from caffeine to cocaine, from shopping to sex, there's something out there, some vice, we cannot leave alone or moderate?

Working with my doctor helped me to finally begin to see myself without anger or recrimination and as just one thing: fully human.

"That's a good place to start," my doctor said flatly, and then pushed me further. We talked more about Rashid and more about Nisa. She met Nisa. She led me to understand that feeling guilty about the breakup or not living up to some fantasy idea of the perfect mother was not going to change past actions. "You can feel guilty all you want, but are you going to get back together with Rashid?" she asked. "I can't see it," I confessed, "not with the deportation order." Admitting that brought me to a greater truth, a good one, if not an easy one.

I couldn't see being with anyone right then. I thought about all the years I'd spent, from fourteen to thirty-seven, involved, engaged, or married. "I feel good about being single, about getting to finally know myself as my own woman, not a woman inexorably bound to a man. I want to know Nisa better too," I said, and then set about the business of making that happen.

Because when I looked at all of it, when I looked back through all of it, I had no choice but this one, this one that required my real sweat and my real, real labor: not only the work of dealing with my own fears and demons, but the work of taking those observations and using them to change long-standing patterns of behavior.

In my own life, the war on terror has not been about distant shores or cultures, not about planes and buildings or suicide bombers. The war on terror was a battleground inside myself that I have fought on and fought on so that I could stand here now—not broken all the way, not broken so much that I can't be pieced back together, not broken to the extent that I would be rendered an ineffective and useless mother to my Nisa, my child, my bright light in the big city. I will never be that broken. I will never come even close to it again.

something like beautiful

It's a Sunday night and I'm thinking, this is it, the reason I did it, the reason I do it. The weekend has been perfect. Even with all of the imperfections in our lives—the locked-away father, the shaky finances, my addictions, my depression—this weekend they do not intrude on us. They do not stop us from being ourselves. They do not stop me from being me; Nisa is always herself.

And it's not as though there was some great incredible happening or happenings this weekend I'm telling you of; we spent one day in bed, ordering pizza, snuggling, watching scary movies. The other day, we baked cupcakes and read to each other and organized ourselves for the week and finished homework and spoke of many things. For nearly two hours on a Saturday, Nisa went on about her friends, whom she loves, whom she has always loved even if they are kind of annoying to her in certain ways (which she sometimes confesses to me really secret-like, pulling me aside, a whisper in my ear). She details who she wants to have sleepovers with and why and what they will do when they are together, and also who understands her because they're an Aries like her.

It is weekends like this, of which there are many, that make me weep from not understanding: why was I ever so sad? Why was I ever in so much pain? Not that there haven't been losses, but for whatever else is gone, now, at long last, I see what is not gone, I see who is not gone.

I see who is right here, right here and grinning and making up bad jokes and running back and forth and helping out with housework and hugging me and asking for just one more kiss as she blows bubbles from her bubble bath around herself and onto me.

Another confession: as hard as it is, there are times like this weekend when I do not mind being a single parent. If I am completely honest, after all of these years out here on my own, I just can't say that I would even know how to share decision making with someone else. After so long figuring out how to do this alone, how would I begin to be a fair coparent? Even with Rashid, I would find it hard. I would do it, of course I would do it, but when I think about it, I think about it in the way you approach figuring out how to win a tug-of-war.

Not that I believe that this is either right or perfect. What I am saying is that while it is not perfect, I do like my life. While it is not perfect, it is something like beautiful, the rhythm we have found, my Nisa and I, the rhythm that we make, just the two of us here, alone, together. Despite my dreams about family, about having bunches of children and a loving husband, I looked up one day and had to come to terms with the fact that we were it, me and Nisa. And we may never be more than this, and that is fine.

But this weekend, like on other weekends before it, none of these thoughts intruded. We were just us, as is, and as is, we traveled. We talked about Halloween, Nisa and I. We talked about Paris and the Mona Lisa and the Louvre. We talked about Malcolm X, the value of good handwriting, the Cheetah Girls, the *Amistad*, the hosing of nonviolent protesters during the civil rights movement, Marie Antoinette and the beginnings of fashion as we know it today. We talked about why one should oppose the death penalty, Mumia Abu-Jamal, what food dye to use to make the cupcakes the right shade of Halloween orange, the difference between granulated and confectioners' sugar, and we talked about medicine; Nisa toys with the idea of becoming a doctor and lately has taken to watching the Discovery Health channel over Disney.

When my baby finally drifts off to sleep and when I finally lie down to do the same, I wonder, with all of this exploration, all of this excitement, all of these big conversations over broad and thick landscapes, landscapes that even seem enchanted in some way, where was there room for depression to creep in?

How did I not see it when it first began, how did I not feel it stretching me open, leaving a canyon of sorrow where there should have been peace? How did I not stop it? Did it happen while I was sleeping, while I was looking the other way, while I was multitasking, punch-drunk with exhaustion, reading the *Times*? Did it happen while I was worried about someone or something else? Did it happen, did I really let it happen on my watch?

And if it did, if all this happened on my watch and if it is not simply my cross to bear, but a cross I allowed and that I willingly offered to carry alone, I want to say I was wrong. I want to say that to Nisa. I want to explain to her that perhaps I have closed away people because after everything, it has felt safer. I want to say I'm sorry I didn't do better. I want to ask for another chance. I want to admit that I cannot imagine loving again. I cannot imagine being in love again. I can't. But being unwilling to love, being unwilling to love as a grown-up woman, that cannot be the answer. It cannot be the model for my child, not for my loving child, not for my child who loves to love.

My eyes are heavy now and I'm drifting off to sleep. I'm drifting and I'm thinking that I want to do better, I want the world to be better for Nisa, better for me. I may not be able to fix the world, reverse global warming, stop child abuse, or change a man whose rage blankets his heart. But I can fix me. I do not want to give in to my fear, my fear that to love is to open yourself up to pain that cannot ever be resolved. Which is why I know that to have more weekends that are just as incredible, we have to open up the door to it, I have to open the door. And to open up the door in ways I haven't done, I should learn from someone who seems to have always known how.

I have to take your lead, Nisa, and not be afraid, not offer only false intimacy, but offer the real thing, real friendships, real love. Like you do.

So when it is late and the dark sky is encompassing and thorough and Nisa is sleeping next to me, I return to the place of peace I once knew. I return with all the humility I can conjure up and call my own, and then I meditate and then I pray for a space to be given, for a space to be opened up to allow in the bringers of light, the dream weavers, the supernovas, the luminous, the pure, the mighty believers in love, the earth angels in our midst, those who do not know how to hate or to reject, who do not know cruelty as an option, those who choose laughter and joy and kindness—mostly that, kindness—again and again and again and again.

I ask them to come.

In the sweet, soft hours I have learned to call on the seers to shore me up, to call on those who have a particular and clear vision and who are all around us and who come through us, even as we have set them aside. It's the children. It's always been the children.

Without empty sentiment or hyperbole, we know this, we really do. We know what children see. We memorialize it in poems, in stories we exchange in the autumn of our years, about our once-upon-a-time innocence, our long-ago goodness before we made whatever decisions that took us out of our ethics, out of ourselves. This is the subject of novels and nonfiction alike, across cultures and generations. So we know. We know.

And just as much, we know what they, the children, are capable of giving us. We pretend that our exchange with them is a one-way street—us changing the diapers or breast-feeding or helping with homework or paying for college. We have a million reasons why they owe us. But when we tell the whole truth, we have to acknowledge what we owe them, which begins with us embracing the beauty and the character most of our children give right back to us, and they give right back to us freely: their tiny bodies appearing seemingly out of nowhere just to say, I love you, Mommy!

And we say that we understand this, we say that we know how important the babies are. We say it in slogans and we say it on T-shirts. We say it on bumper stickers and politicians say it on the campaign trail. Parents and educators say it in the PTA. And I know many of us mean it when the words spill out of our mouths. The problem is that we just don't act on it. Not en masse, not as a movement. We have to be a movement even if we start a movement within our own singular hearts.

If we do, if we are, schools across this nation will rise up from the physical and academic shambles. No child will ever die of an impacted tooth because somehow Medicaid's paperwork and an insurance company's paperwork mattered more than a young life, mattered more than life itself, which is why even with a mother on the phone almost daily, begging and begging to please help her baby, still watched that boy die waiting for someone to approve the needed surgery, died because the poison traveled up from his tooth and into his brain and he was twelve, just twelve years old in 2007, when it went down just like that. And it would not have happened if we put power behind the platitudes, muscle behind the musings.

Chemicals would not be dumped into specific neighborhoods so that all the babies wake up one Harlem morning with asthma. Childbirth would not still be—as it was in the thirteenth century—the leading cause of death for women. Rape would not still be pandemic and the majority of rapes would not occur before a child is eighteen, with half of those occurring before a child is twelve. The infant mortality rate in Mississippi would not have doubled almost exclusively because of Clinton's welfare-reform policy, which has made getting prenatal care almost impossible for the poorest of mothers.

We would not hire more police to stem the flow of urban violence. If the police could fix the problem, there wouldn't be so many jails and prisons, a back-end solution to a problem that is best addressed head-on, in the way of G. Asenath Andrews, principal of the Catherine Ferguson Academy in Detroit, a school for pregnant and parenting girls, children normally left at the bottom of the list when their names are mentioned at all. Under her leadership, ninety percent graduate from high school. And one hundred percent of those are accepted to college. We would turn to her, and we would ask her to help us develop a curriculum that is meaningful in our own children's lives. We would listen to her because she listens and pays attention to young people. We'd listen to her or else we would listen to Mad Dads or Barrios Unidos, the people on the ground who honor our children, put their lives on the line for our future's sake. We would listen to them over the voices of the screaming mad men and women on talk radio shows, on Fox News. We would listen to our own children. I am trying to listen to my own children, the one I made, the ones in my universe.

Which is not to say that children know all, or see or understand all. But the breadth of the integrity most of them embody and are willing to share with the world, until we talk or beat or trick or lie or neglect them out of it, the genuine space of love and truth in their hearts that is so readily and easily accessible, and their real curiosity, and their true push to do better, be better—I know that these are the qualities too often missing from the adult world I inhabit. We would listen to them, our children, and right now we do not.

We listen nearly exclusively to those who have the right title, or the right figure in their bank account, sometimes just the right look. But all those things, which admittedly I have coveted in my life—good looks, money, position—I know now, after everything, that I can live without them, without the kind of money I once strove for and without the stature I once thought essential and Lord knows I can live with not being the prettiest, but I will not survive without what my daughter brings to me each good morning: love, spiritual excellence, integrity. And gratitude.

So yes, in the quiet hours, I say it and I say it and then I say it again: Come, Nisa.

Come, Nina and Naima and Adasa and Jahiya.

Come, Lauren and Spencer and Mark and Aanisah.

Come, Zakiyah and Adisa and Eleni and Monifa, little Asha and Zioni and Truth; come, Eva.

Come, Aja and Butterfly and Petricia and Brianna.

Come, Nico; come, Sule; come, Lucas; come, Charlie and Simone.

Come, Adana and Zuri and Arian and Amina and Amina.

Come, Tuari. Bring your brother. Come, Brooks, bring your sister; come, Aljameer, and come, Aundre.

Come, Karin and Justine, Brittany J. and Diamond.

Come, you all, everyone.

Come, let all of us see you. Let you see yourself, and then let every one of us who needs it be able to finally truly see ourselves and begin to heal.

motherhood, lost and found

I t's Thanksgiving weekend and I am telling Anne the story, the real story, the one I have lived, the one I have denied. For years my sister has stood alongside me steadfast and faithful, waiting and asking, "Sister, when is Rashid coming home? What's happening with his case?" For years I have answered these inquiries sort of *Rashomon*-like, telling pieces of what's happening, small corners of the nightmare, letting her put her own spin on whatever I shared.

But I want to claim my life now, for all that it has been and all that it has not been, and I tell Anne this. This is my one life, I say to her. I want to have it and have it fully, no matter what that means.

We have returned to my Brooklyn apartment from our mother's home, the home we grew up in. And we are, for all the stumbling and stuttering and missteps and mishaps, grown and sexy women now, possessed of all that that means:

We have a past—lost or found loves, bruises that still show and wounds that have healed.

We have a present—families and debt and decisions about schools, irritations on the job.

And we have a future, three children between us—my gorgeous, sometimes sulky, and teenaged niece, Lauren; my nephew, Spencer, a boy's boy, who bounces off walls, falls out of trees. He was born six months before Nisa. And we have Nisa.

She has left me and my sister in the living room, and has taken her cousin Spencer by the hand and led him down my long hallway to where the bedrooms are. Warren, my brother-in-law, jet-lagged and exhausted, is asleep in my bed and I tell the children not to wake him, not to go into my room. They say okay, and they do not break their promise, but later, when my sister and I wander down the hallway to check on our babies, who are dangerously quiet, we discover Spencer and Nisa have pulled out what appears to be every last toy Nisa has ever owned and barricaded them against my bedroom door. We shake our heads, my sister and I, decide there has been no harm done— Warren's slept through the whole thing—and we return to the living room. We return to the comfort and familiarity of our sisterhood.

Watching all of our children expand in and explore the universe of each of their lives is how she gets me to talk, slowly at first but then with urgency. Anne comments simply but emphatically that she doesn't know how I do it, the single-mother thing. "I know it's common," she says, "so people think it's easy, but honestly, I don't know how you do it."

It is true, I tell her. It's hard, despite how common it is, it's impossibly hard. I have hated—I guess I still hate—having to be the sole emotional and financial provider for my daughter. The pressure is too great, I explain. The idea that if you slip, no one will be there to catch you and, worse, no one will be there to catch your baby—it's a responsibility you can neither fully handle nor ever shirk.

So, yes, yes, I say finally to my sister, somewhere between potty training, playdates, speaking engagements, bylines, and balancing the household books, I lost pieces of myself I am only now trying to reclaim.

And no, I told her, no there wasn't a way I could hold together my marriage.

The deportation order meant that for Rashid and me to have a future, not only would I have to reposition my entire life once again, but I would have to do the same for Nisa. What may have been fair for me, a choice I made for myself as a girl of twenty-three who fell in love, is not a choice I can make for my unsuspecting daughter: shock uprooting. But even before the deportation order, I could remember during the first months of Nisa's life how caring for Rashid and Nisa at the same time was far more than I could bear.

I told her about the weekly treks through metal detectors and bars, the parts of your spirit that always seemed to get snagged by the razor-wire that's just everywhere—I couldn't keep doing it. I will never keep Nisa from knowing her father, but for me to be romantically entangled with him now, when I need him most and yet most feel his absence, is just too painful. But every second I see Nisa grow, change, fall down, stand up again, is a second I am reminded that the only other person who loves her as I do, is not there to be a witness.

When I became a mother, I thought Rashid's absence would be all about needing someone to help carry the groceries into the house or cover the utilities bill. But the worst part of it all, the part that chokes in my throat, is that I have no one with whom to share the everyday beauty and wonder of my child. No one who will ever lose an hour of time, as I still regularly do, just watching her sleep.

We want the world to see and share in all that we are proud of, our beautiful homes, hairstyles, jewelry, cars. How could I live with the fact that my husband embodied the idea that there was both someone and no one to witness her with me, raise a hand and testify, speak in tongues about the most beautiful thing we could ever have, ever hope to have?

I couldn't play at house or marriage anymore. I confessed to my sister that that's what I said to Rashid finally. I think I said, "I need the real thing or I need to woman up and just do this on my own."

But that breakup left me with a grief so profound, it has no name I can call. It felt akin to losing my husband, best friend, father, and brother on the very same day. Not losing them so much as sending them away, banishing them. They vanished by my own hand. And for that, I may never be able to forgive myself. But I had to choose my child. Again.

Anne asks if I think he will ever come home, come home to me and to Nisa, and would I be willing to try with him again? I hesitate, searching for the honest answer to the question that stalks behind me. "I can't see it," I tell her. "But I have a hard time seeing any relationship right now beyond the one with myself and the one with Nisa," I say, and then quickly add, "She loves her dad very much, though. They're on the phone all the time." I explain as tears begin to form in my eyes. But before they have a chance to go ahead and push for real, my sister and

I have dissolved into laughter, dissolved into our lives, as Warren discovers the barricade, bellows out from the bedroom in complete confusion, *Hey, what's going on?!* And two small children stand triumphant and grinning alongside us, their mothers.

⟡

My head is in my sister's lap and the toys have been put away. Nisa and Spencer are quiet in her room and Warren is still lying down in mine. Who knew we would get here, Anne and I, born of different wombs, different gene pools, yet sisters all the same, close as any two sisters ever were. We always said we wanted to be pregnant together. We were. We always said I should be there when Spencer was born. Her original due date—in January of 2000—was not one on which I could arrange travel. On my last visit before the baby was born, we fretted about this but made the best of it, and early in the morning on November 25, 1999, while I was cleaning and chopping greens for the holiday meal, my sister's water broke. She was five weeks early. As things turned out, I was right there for Spencer's birth, the first to feed him as he lay, tiny at 4.8 pounds, in NICU.

And when I look at him now, this rough, big old boy, and I remember those hours in the hospital and the fears that gripped all of us before Spencer was born and safe. I thought I would always remember everything, every moment of pregnancy, every moment with my child, with our children. I was so sure that each kick, each change in my body, would permanently implant itself in the most accessible part of my memory.

Childbirth cured me of that fallacy, but only briefly.

Once Nisa was born it seemed impossible that I would be

unable to record and repeat, years and years on, well into my old age, each second of her life. She was developing brilliantly and everything she did touched my heart so! How could these memories, defining as they were, ever, ever fade?

Each phase was miraculous to me and I never wanted us to leave it. I wanted to watch her discover her hands and toes again and again. Or the day she pushed herself up onto all fours and began to rock back and forth, a two-day precursor to the afternoon she began to crawl. Her first solid food (a strawberry at my friend and agent Victoria's dinner party—Nisa snatched it out of my plate and worked on it and worked on it, an hour it seemed, until she conquered that thing. She still loves strawberries). Her first step ever, when she was eight months old, in my office's conference room.

But for every memory embedded, for every memory that is there, sitting in my hands for me to hold close, there are scads more I have forgotten. With each phase I thought I could not get past, that I wanted to live in with Nisa forever, the truth was that the next one that came proved just as enchanting.

Parenting is not one moment or ten moments. It's not one year or five years. It's the whole thing, all the moments and years added up together. It's a lifetime. It's a lifetime of perfection, a lifetime of error. It's a lifetime of starting and stopping, getting it wrong, then getting it right, then getting it wrong again, but never once thinking that quitting is an option. It's about doing what so many of us never learn to do in any other relationship— what I had not learned how to do—to keep coming back, keep showing up, keep trying harder. Keep doing it and doing it.

When I finally got that about my own parenting, when I finally stopped trapping myself in one or ten bad decisions, and realized that Nisa and I would be a lifetime of decisions, a relationship that was going to keep unfolding, I finally understood my own parents, who are doing this lifetime with me. They are the ones who kept coming back and back. They are the ones who chose the relationship and then stayed with it, no matter how hard. And it's what I realize about the mother I never knew, the one who didn't do a moment with me. She didn't choose me. She didn't choose the work of a relationship with me. I may never fully recover from that. I may never fully *move on*. But now, all these years in, when I look into my daughter's face and see myself staring back and feel this great love, this great connective tissue, the DNA of it, but more the soul of it, the lifetime we are sharing, I know that when I look into my parents' faces, my sister's, the same connection is there.

We are not blood of the same blood, flesh of the same flesh. And necessarily Spencer and Nisa are not either. But even with three thousand miles between them, you will not meet two cousins more close. You will not meet two people more family, through and through.

The instruction that I, me the woman without a bloodline, have received simply watching these two small children born as a century turned over along with nations and belief systems and much of what we thought we knew for sure, has been more healing for me than even the therapy.

I tell my sister this on that night when we are all together and she is asking me questions that only my little sister could ask me. I tell her about going through labor—I had natural childbirth outside a hospital setting. For me labor was less about pain than it was discomfort and it was the most incredible experience of my life. It was the one time that I was so focused on something that my mind never wandered. It stayed right there, on what I had to do: bring that baby forward safely.

Every other experience in my life, no matter how intense, always caused me to lose focus at some point. Great sex, great conversations, a great movie, working out, or writing—at some point my mind drifts. The twelve hours I spent in labor, and in particular the five I spent in hard labor, allowed nothing else into the space.

That's sort of how I want to be as a mother: fully engaged. Fully present. Not every second, of course. Of course I want and need time for myself and I take it, at the gym, with a small circle of close friends. But when it is time for me to be with Nisa, I don't want to do it looking the other way. I don't want to do it texting on my BlackBerry or chatting about nothing on a cell phone.

I spent so much of my life flying to different cities, being with different people, and all the while only half-present, all the while just wanting to be back at home. If I add up all the years I didn't pay attention to what I was experiencing, what I was living, I may have handed away a decade, maybe more. I don't want to hand over another second.

So when it is just us, more often than not my phones are turned off now, and even when the day is a little gray, so we have to stay inside and read books or play cards and watch movies and snuggle, it's fine. It's fine and we can do this all day, play-ing cards and dancing to Santana, Destiny's Child, and Hannah Montana. We can do it and feel it to be as much of an adventure as climbing mountains in distant lands. But for all those adventures, where we live is a place we can pull the sun toward our center and fashion color out of dark, possibility out of despair, and then shine, we do, a mother and daughter, together but also separately, the two us, a team, alchemists stirring a pot of secret ingredients and turning out gold.

And as I lurch toward the end of this crippling period of depression, it occurs to me that the one thing I will not rush through is motherhood. With all that has hurt and with all that has been hard, I would take every second one more time over, two more times over, if it meant I would do it with my Nisa again.

I review once more the last several years. This is when it washes over me, the sense of hope, the immensity of the great beauty that graced my life, my life as a mother. I think about how with each and every sunrise we begin the process of re-creation, recasting, reordering, and reinventing. We begin our days on our knees, with our fingers in the dirt. We are planting, Nisa and I, ideas and possibilities. And trees. We are planting trees because in parts of Africa they say when something dies you plant a tree and something did die, a certain and particular vision of tomorrow, and so we plant a tree, our family tree and all that it means.

Because in between everything, the breakups, the letdowns, the entire days I suspected I might have fallen over the cliff into complete mental illness, in between those moments and the deadlines, Nisa and I find ways to travel, as we do to this day, to places far and wide, in New York City, in small towns and big cities across the country, in big cities and small towns outside of the country. Poetry readings, conferences, family gatherings, and sometimes even vacations, we find ways to make this world our own.

And wherever we are, we gaze with amazement at the differences each place has offered: the wide deserts just below the snowcapped mountains of Southern California; the forever redwoods in the north; the mighty mountains in the Berkshires; the ready dance, blues and hues of Chi-Town; the swaying palms and rainbow fish of Sanibel Island; the alligators and swamplands of South Carolina and the hot, wet, greener than green of Mississippi; the unimaginable width of the Texas sky; the see-through waters of the Caribbean Sea; the mighty beauty of the Sierra Madres, where mountaintops touch the clouds and where we stood beneath waterfalls; the great sperm whales moving through the waters that hold the Grenadines, with the grace of a creature far smaller.

And all that color and life everywhere, including in the parks and gardens of urban landscapes like our own—we lose ourselves in it, Nisa and I do. We lose ourselves there and in art galleries and museums, in Marsalis's jazz and 50's rhymes, in movies and on Broadway, at the ice-cream stand in the summertime and our sushi spot all year long. We make intricate plans for the trips we have not yet taken together to see the endless lights of Paris; the Eastern Cape of South Africa where Mandela played as a child and Biko struggled as a man; Santorini on her next birthday so we can discover whether the azalea plants are as impossibly pink as and taller than the ones on Kos; and Bora-Bora, so different from all we know, so far away, that we can only imagine it as a land of dragons, unicorns, mermaids, and stardust.

Nisa wants to climb the volcano I climbed in Costa Rica four months before I became pregnant with her. I promise her we will do that trip, and also one to Baja some January during the migration of the pregnant gray whales. If I have to tell the truth, the whole of it, then yes, yes, there were times of utter despair, but even on those days, even then, we embraced it, this life; we have bathed ourselves in it, and we have retained our memories in stories we whisper to each other when it's late and dark but we want, still, to hang on.

When I have thought I was losing everything, every part of my mind, what has brought me back to truth is Nisa, the force of her life. That and learning to rediscover the beauty of living itself by watching my daughter seek out life everywhere and claim it. It is too much responsibility to put on a child, I know, and I swear I didn't do it on purpose, but it is how it went down, me witnessing her, watching her, it carried me through moments when I thought I had lost all my endurance.

Most mornings I am awakened by her laughter and then the inevitable messy kisses planted on my cheek. Her eyes ablaze with mischief, wonder, excitement, and hope, Nisa's query to me each sunrise is the same: "What's our big adventure today, Mommy?"

I grin back at my beloved, *my* child, and my mind begins to work. But before I come up with a plan, this is what I think each time she asks: *Yes, Beloved. Our big adventure, indeed. Ours.*

acknowledgments

When you finally sit, assume the position, and start doing it, writing the life can sometimes seem actually more challenging than living the life. I can argue either point of view in equal measure, depending on the demands of the day. But whichever sentiment is true, what I know is that neither the living nor writing occurs in its best form without the love, wisdom, and camaraderie of the people who've chosen to stand beside us.

In my own life, particular acknowledgment must be made to the women who, in varying ways, taught me invaluable lessons about being a mother: first, my own mom, Dolores Bullard, and my sister, Anne Coleman. But also the women closest to me: Autumn Amberbridge, Kimberly Elise, Qamara Clark, Susan Taylor, Myrian Tooma, Robin Templeton, dream hampton, Monifa Bandele and her mom, Marie Murray.

There are many men who've shared their hearts with my

daughter and me as well. Two who've especially done so will always have my love, Nisa's love, and unending appreciation: George Caros and Stanley Crouch.

Nora (Stewart) Alexis has helped me care for my daughter so fully for so long and with so much love, I was able not only to write but to grow these last hard years. Thank you.

Audrey Edwards and Robin Stone read early versions of what finally became this book. I am deeply grateful for their editing, counsel, friendship, and lessons in parenting.

Former colleagues at *Essence* magazine and current ones at the Drug Policy Alliance have continually circled my daughter with love the countless times I have needed to file a story or a report with her at my side. We cannot thank you enough.

I don't know an author who can navigate any part of the journey without a fine editor. I am lucky enough to be, eleven years on, still working with the best among us, Gillian Blake. For both the push and the patience, I am forever grateful.

Finally, and for more than I will ever, ever be able to list, my great, great gratitude—and still love after all these years— is reserved for Zayd Rashid, who I hope will one day walk a Brooklyn neighborhood, hand in hand, with our daughter.

For him, for Nisa, for the now millions of children and parents who are divided by bars and barbed wire, your day— unrestricted and unrestrained—will come.

about the author

asha bandele is the author of four books, including the award-winning memoir *The Prisoner's Wife*. A Columbia University Revson Fellow (2004–2005) and former *Essence* magazine features editor, asha's work has been published in numerous outlets, including the *New York Times*, *Vibe*, *The Source*, *Family Circle*, and *Huffington Post*. Aside from writing, asha also directs a grants program for the Drug Policy Alliance, the nation's leading organization fighting the war on drugs. She holds degrees from the New School for Social Research and Bennington College and lives in Brooklyn, New York, where she is raising her daughter, Nisa.